WOUNDED HEALER

Cover Photo Design by Xcellence Publications LLC
Layout & Copyright by Xcellence Publications LLC

Edited By Donna R. Patrick & Co-Authors

Printed and Bounding by:
Banner Digital Printing and Publishing, Inc

Publishing Company
Xcellence Publications LLC
1-877-382-8125
Copyright: 1-10303790161
ISBN: 978-0-692-90045-1

Contact Higher Ground
yp@higherground55.com
P.O. Box 603456
Cleveland, Ohio 44103

TABLE OF CONTENTS

CO-AUTHORS

CONTRIBUTING WRITERS

CONTRIBUTING WRITERS (CONT.)

I will never leave you nor will I ever forsake you.

- Joshua 1:5

FORWARD

by
Shelley Shockley

Gather together, sisters. Arms open wide. Fingertips touching, your stance mimics the live Oak. Welcome is the message you confer to those coming after you. Wounded Healer offers words of encouragement and understanding, much like a shoulder you can lean into as you release the boulder you have been carrying.

We wrap you in our embrace while encouraging you to release your burdens and cares. Within these pages, you will find a safe space, a place to hear the voices of your sisters, understanding the path they have traveled. Feel the pain, the struggle, despair, but most importantly, the joy and triumph. A healing balm is offered to you as reassurance that you, too, can conquer your trials.

Wounded, yes. Defeated, not in the least. Each of these stories reflects a portion of a journey. It represents the resilience found in each writer. These shoulders are the weeping walls on which your cares are meant to lie.

Innately, we seek shelter from harm, just as from infancy, when we sought our mother's bosom and her wisdom. As we grew, we shared our secrets with that best friend we met in elementary school or that favorite cousin we spent every weekend with. Those friends and cousins became our confidantes, and depending on your family structure; it may have been that favorite auntie, grandmother, or even grandfather. Always, there was someone you could bounce ideas off, cry about your hurts, then at some point, we looked in the mirror and said I have to handle this myself. At that point, your troubles manifested because instead of giving it to God or someone you trusted, you struggled alone.

As social beings, we innately navigated to others, but did you know that this is scientifically known to aid your mental health? Investigators have argued that rich social networks may reduce the rate at which individuals engage in risky behaviors, prevent negative appraisals, and increase treatment adherence. In general, resilient or hardy individuals are thought to use active coping mechanisms when dealing with stressful life situations. Additionally, our bodies are equipped with the hormone oxytocin produced by the hypothalamus and secreted by the pituitary gland, which works in conjunction with social support to reduce the impact of stress and trauma.

Robyn Hill, a Cleveland Licensed Professional Clinical Counselor (LPCC), also stresses the need for interpersonal relationships to heal after suffering traumatic situations. She said, "In interpersonal neurobiology, it is necessary to heal to be in the community." She also noted that the current pandemic and prior to that our reliance on electronic devices is affecting our mental health, stating, "Our society is lacking connective mass particularly with social media, and even more so with Covid-19."

This book is a testament to that circle of love that will engulf you because when you do, as the late great Michael Jackson sang, "Look at the Man in the Mirror," the image is of one who has been wounded as well. The question you must ask is, "Will I allow my wound to fester or reach out for help to heal?"

I will make an assumption; the title of this book spoke to you. You are seeking answers on how to heal. While these women don't give you a playbook on healing, they allow you inside their pain. They shed the masks that we as women wear daily. Our worlds are crashing around us, but the face we offer to the public is one of strength. Everything is fine. Inside your stomach, performs gymnastic flips that would make Simone Biles proud. Your mind is racing, and you don't know when or where your answer will reveal itself.

The first step is releasing and giving your troubles to God. If you're unsure of how to do this, read Philippians 4:6, "Do not be anxious about anything, but in every situation, by prayer and petition, with thanksgiving, present your requests to God." I have learned from reading His word that your answer will come in many ways. We often hear people testify, "God told me to do it."

That is not always a voice from above; it may come in the form of a family member, friend, or confidant.

The stories within these pages are of women who believed, but maybe their faith was wavering. I believe God placed individuals in their lives to help them through their trials. I know He has done it for me, and He can do it for you too.

Use this text as a guide to help you over that bridge to your greatness. Each of these women recognized they are not on this journey alone. First, and foremost our Father is with them always, and it never hurts to have some women and men who love the Lord in your corner. It is my prayer that something within these pages resonates with you and leads you forward; it is also the prayer of the co-authors of this publication, Dr. Yvonne Pointer, Jacqueline Payne, Jacqueline Muhammad.

These three women came together in hopes that allowing women to share their testimonies with others proves that wounds can heal and be used to help others. May God continue to bless them and their visions.

May God continue to bless you on your journey. He has brought you this far, and He will not leave you, "As I was with Moses, so I will be with you; I will never leave you nor forsake you," Joshua 1:5.

Two are better than one, because they have a good return for their work: If one falls down, his friend can help him up. But pity the man who falls and has no one to help him up! Also, if two lie down together, they will keep warm. But how can one keep warm alone? Though one may be overpowered two can defend themselves. A cord of three strands is not quickly broken.
Ecclesiastes 4:9-12

INTRODUCTION

Growing up in a family of ten children (nine in Cleveland one brother in Chicago) in the inner city was often tough. Life always seemed crowded, forcing me at times to scammer in search of my own identity. I was a solemn, introverted child and could often be found hiding with my face buried inside a book. I yearned to escape, to find a place like Dorothy in the Wizard of Oz, somewhere over the rainbow. I wanted a place where there were rolling hills and beautiful fields of blooming flowers, a habitat where sorrow and pain were nonexistent. However, there wasn't such a place, at least not in the life of this little girl on Hough Avenue.

How it was that even as a child, I knew such a place existed? It might be best defined in a comment made to me a few years ago by my mother, LuElla Pointer. The matriarch of ten children, who recently passed away, may not physically be with us anymore, but her words linger in the confines of my mind like a scratched record repeating the same tune. "Yvonne," she said, "You scare me because you talk straight to God." Her comments were based on her observation of my ongoing conversations with God, even as a child.

As a little girl, I was once given the assignment to see after a younger sibling. While under my care, he was playing with a ball and jacks, he placed one of the jacks in his mouth, and it became lodged in his throat. The entire family raced back and forth in a fit of panic and desperation while waiting for the ambulance to transport him to the hospital. They were all panicking.

Everyone was panicking except me! I knew exactly what to do as I walked calmly past them all to the foot of my bed and knelt in prayer. My request was loud enough for them to hear, yet simple: "Lord, please don't let my brother die," I asked. Needless to say, he survived. This was my earliest recollection of the power of prayer and my realization that I could go to God for help. I had someone bigger than I, and over the years, my mother made the same observation.

Following the December 6, 1984, brutal rape and murder of my fourteen-year-old daughter, Gloria Pointer, I would spend endless hours alone in the sanctuary of my church. My mother's question to me was, "what in the world do you do all day long in there by yourself, for so many hours every day?" My response was simply, I talk to God. Yvonne, you scare me," is all she would say. I know the sound of God's voice and the deafening sound of His silence. At times it is bewildering how vivid and descriptive God can be. At times, his instructions are as loud as the clanging of a bell summoning me to the dinner table and at other times as soft as a whisper or a gentle breeze. It was during one of those times as I sat in the prayer room of my home, affectionately called the Hope Haven. In this comforting location where I pray early every morning for twenty-four minutes, I heard the following words, "WOUNDED HEALER.... WRITE A BOOK!"

What followed the words were specific instructions! As an author and an avid reader, I know all too well the power of written words, words that can transport a person from despair to destiny! During that morning prayer, God reminded me of a specific time in my life when I could go no further, a time when all hope seems to have perished, and I needed the help of someone. And just like that, when this student was ready, a teacher appeared. God sent help. A reassuring presence, a guide, and a friend. Often that help comes from a person who has traveled the road previously, someone who knows the pitfalls and the dangers up ahead, someone who has escaped the travesties of life but has never forgotten the way. It is someone who has been bruised and scarred along the way but is willing to go back and help another. That someone becomes a HEALER to the Wounded. They realize that their life is not their own, and they have an obligation to go back. Even as I type these words, I am reminded of women like Harriet Tubman. I would describe her as the ultimate Wounded Healer because she returned in spite of her own WOUNDS. She is an example for others to follow.

So, maybe my mother was right. I do talk to God, but not only that - God talks back to me. His specific instructions were to gather women who would share their stories and place them into the pages of this book. They would be stories of how they were able to survive because someone helped them cross over the bridge; because someone took the time to bandage their wounds and give them a shoulder to lean on. After hearing God's instructions, my first course of action was to solicit the help of two of my dearest confidants, Jacqueline Payne and Jacqueline Muhammad. We had worked together successfully in the past on numerous God projects, and I knew that an assignment of this magnitude could use their affirming and reassuring hands.

So, we began the process of personally selecting the incredible women who would share their testimonies. Many of them had never uttered these words of deliverance before the publication of this book. With that said, journey with us; take our hands as we escort you through the stories of my co-authors and twenty-four incredibly brave contributing writers, who demonstrate that there is HEALING hope for you and that it just might come from the WOUNDS of others.

Dr. Yvonne Pointer

CO- AUTHORS

Dr. Yvonne Pointer

Yvonne Pointer can best be described as a Community Activist, Philanthropist, Humanitarian, Author, national and international Speaker. Her fourteen- year-old daughter, Gloria Pointer, was brutally raped and murdered in 1984. Her daughter's homicide was eventually solved after a twenty-nine- year search for the killer. She is a firm believer that one person can make a difference and that we must be the change that we would like to see in the world. She is the founder of Positive Plus, a self-help support group for women. She also founded Higher Ground Speakers Bureau and supported the Gloria Pointer Teen Movement in Ghana, West Africa.

For more information about Dr. Pointer, visit www.YvonnePointer.com

A ROSE IS STILL A ROSE

Dr. Yvonne Pointer

Have you ever had something so devastating happen to you in life that it felt as if the bottom of the world had been pulled from beneath you? Something so horrific that the very will to live was stripped from your soul? Well, I did! On December 6, 1984, my fourteen-year-old daughter, Gloria Pointer, was brutally raped and murdered. This one catastrophic occurrence has forever changed my life.

Despite the brutality of the crime, I somehow found strength by God's grace to conduct numerous national and local media appearances. You see, I had promised Gloria while standing over her casket that the person who murdered her would be captured. I needed the media's help because there was still a killer loose in the city. I eventually became a much sought- after spokeswoman pertaining to child safety and victimization. Yes, on the outside, I appeared to be a pillar of strength; but behind closed doors, I was unable to function. The simple task of fixing dinner, doing laundry, or caring for my other two children was insurmountable. I would hide behind the closed door of my bedroom, longing for my life to come to an end just as my daughter's had.

How was it even possible to function behind the death of a child? How could life continue moving forward when my life had come to a screeching end? It was then that my Sistah Friend, Rose Starks, came to my rescue like a superwoman faster than a speeding locomotive. Rose and I attended the same church, and we were both single parents. We often cried on each other's shoulders when life got too hard. We shared meals and would babysit for each other. We were more than friends; we were Sistahs! When Gloria was murdered, it was Rose who mothered not only her own children but mine as well. She literally moved into my house and remained for nine months, doing for my family and me what we could not do for ourselves. However, when the cameras were on, I could sit upright and regal; but afterward, I spiraled back into the depths of depression.

Did I mention that Rose was also battling a crippling illness? She had some type of horrible disease that was hereditary. Many nights from behind my bedroom door, I could hear her weeping and moaning from the unbearable pain that would often cause her to pass out for days. I would never have made it without Rose! She eventually moved to California, and we became long-distance Sistahs. Very often, late-night phone calls and prayers seemed to ease the distance between us. On several occasions, I would visit her in California. Our children were now grown, and we would laugh the night away as we debated over who's grandchildren were the greatest. She never complained about her sickness, but I could often hear the weakness in her voice.

Eventually, cancer had spread to all of her organs, including her brain. I went to visit her, and she was frail and barely able to stand. My heart broke for this wounded healer, SISTAH FRIEND, who had done so much for me. I felt helpless. When I arrived at her apartment, she was ashamed that it was not as clean as she would like it to be. She offered to pay for me to stay at a hotel, but I refused. I was not going to leave her side. She even sent her son to the store to get fresh towels and linen for the guest bedroom. Rose, a meticulous housekeeper in her heyday, was embarrassed by the way that the spare room was untidy. She said she would sleep on the couch.

Once again, I refused to leave her side. She slept on one end and me on the other. The painful sounds that she made throughout the night kept both of us awake. Eventually, I dozed off but was awakened by the smell of food cooking. I was shocked to see Rose, barely standing against the stove, making me breakfast. I was scheduled to leave that morning, and she wanted to do one last thing for me before I departed. We both knew that this would be our last visit. We prayed and cried and had to be pried apart.

One week later, Rose went to glory! I know that she is no longer here physically, but there are times when I can almost hear her in my thoughts speaking words of encouragement during my difficult days. Not even death could separate the love of a wounded healer like Rose; because at the end of the day, ROSE IS STILL ROSE, even in her absence.

She may not be still here physically, but my love and appreciation for her will live on forever.

Jacqueline Payne

Jacqueline Payne is a wife and mother who is passionate about helping others. She began her career at the Cleveland Metropolitan School District, moving her way to Supervisor Community Initiatives and then Dean of Culture & Engagement. It is where she developed a desire to help grassroots organizations. She started her not-for-profit work as About God's Business in 2007, focusing on the development of grassroots programs. Her commitment to serving in the community-led her to Cuyahoga Community College. While obtaining her Associates in Urban Studies, she also attended Cleveland State University in a dual program. She graduated from Cleveland State University, Maxine Goodman Levin College of Urban Affairs, Organizational Leadership – Bachelors of Arts (Magna Cum Laude (2014). Golden Key, International Honour Society, inducted Jacqueline in 2013.

In 2018, she graduated with honors from Walden University with, Master of Science degree in Human Resource Management. In 2019, Walden University inducted Jacqueline into the National Society of Leadership and Success.

Jacqueline currently provides administrative and human resource services to small businesses and non-profits. She is an active member and partner at Redeeming Love Christian Church, Conyers, GA, where she serves along-side the Co-Pastor as Armor-Bearer, the Women's Ministry, and as an Intercessor.

To contact Jacqueline, email agodsb55@gmail.com

WHAT ARE YOU EXPECTING?

Jacqueline Payne

Sometimes our journey's weight becomes so heavy that we can no longer move forward the way we have in the past. In a troubling season, there can be grief, financial hardship, and sickness. When we think we are strong, these things can catapult us into a place of weakness. I am reminded of a scripture that says, "For in the time of trouble He shall hide me in His pavilion: in the secret of His tabernacle shall He hide me; He shall set me upon a rock" (Psalms 27:5). But what if at the time of trouble, you can't think straight, you can't remember your name, let alone the promises of God. One day trouble found me; at that time, all I wanted was for someone to rescue me from the fear I was feeling.

God has chosen someone specifically for a particular time in your journey. He knows the plan, and He knows our exact location in life. I once saw a caterpillar that at first seemed to be a pesky little insect. I knocked him off the porch banister, down to the ground. As I stood on the porch with two friends, we continued our conversation. The same caterpillar appeared again on the porch railing within minutes. This time it was as if he was making a scene; he wanted us to see him. The elusive caterpillar stretched his body out as far as he could as he moved down the porch railing. It was as if he had somewhere to be and needed us to know we could not stop him from his journey. Maybe he was close to the next phase of his life and could not give up.

If I could have been like the caterpillar when the doctor said it was cancer, I would have removed that ton of bricks off my back. I would have gotten up off the floor and stretched my hands out to the Father. Unlike the caterpillar, I couldn't seem to pull myself up off the floor. The bible was right there on my table; my prayer closet was just a few steps away, but I didn't have the strength to move. God... I screamed as loud as I could!

That was a fall day in October 2016; I remember the sun was shining, as it usually did in Georgia. We had finally made the move that we talked about for years. Moving from freezing Ohio to hot Atlanta was our dream; we would have longer summers and travel to other sunshiny states close to Georgia. These were just a few things on our bucket list that my husband and I looked forward to doing. What was not on my list was receiving a phone call from the doctor saying that I had an aggressive stage three thyroid cancer. As fast as I received that call, that is how quickly the breath was knocked out of my body. Maybe that is how the caterpillar felt when it was knocked off the railing onto the ground. I could feel my body go numb as all the oxygen left my lungs. At that very moment, I fell to the floor, crying out to God from the depths of my soul!

In the next few weeks, my life was on a fast track to address the report I dreaded for more than thirty-six years. Yes, it was thirty-six years ago when I last heard those words, "You have cancer." It was in 1980; back then, I was only fifteen and did not understand what that meant. I could see the seriousness in my mother's eyes, who was my Earth Angel during that time. She carried my pain; she held me up and protected me from the fear of knowing I could die. Although; she tried to protect me, the experience was dreadful, and all I knew was I never wanted to experience it again.

Now the cancer was back for a second time, and I was not a child. The thought of hearing those words again brought on a spirit of fear and uncertainty that I had never felt before. Questions began to flow through my mind like a waterfall. All I could say was, "God! You Promised!" My soul was crushed, and at that moment, I fell on my face crying out to God. Although I was struggling, I knew that the healing I needed could only come from Him. The weeks ahead of me were far from what I had ever imagined. My schedule changed to blood tests, x-rays, CT scans, PET scans, and more blood tests. It was a fast track to deal with what they had diagnosed as aggressive cancer. My husband was my rock, but I was so far away from my first wounded healer, my mom, Viola. It just seems in times like this; you need your mom. During my first cancer experience, my mom would travel by bus to the hospital every day for over a month. She would be at my bedside before I woke up. Now that I am a mother, I know exactly why she was trying to carry my cross. It was her faith in God that got her through each day. Unfortunately, during some wilderness seasons in your life, some people will not be there with you. They can only go so far. We have to go farther, and during this part of the journey, we have to go alone.

Although the road ahead of me appeared to be dark, God was with me. Two months earlier, I met a wonderful and amazing lady. At that time, neither she nor I knew that she was on a God-assignment. Her name is Claretha Ector, also known to me as "Mama Cookie." Claretha came into my life just when God planned. It was like the caterpillar on the porch railing; you have to go where God has destined for you to go. We moved to Georgia in June and were supposed to go by her home when we first arrived. Imagine just moving to a new state and popping up over someone's house you don't know. To us, it seemed inappropriate, so we did not go. After a month, they reached out to us by phone with urgency. "We were asked to watch out for you two, and we have not seen you all yet." Those were the words from Claretha's husband, Moses. My husband and I promised the Ector's we would be there on the upcoming Sunday. From that day forward, we rarely missed Sunday family time at the Ector's.

During the darkest time of my battle with thyroid cancer, Claretha became more than my friend; she became "Mama Cookie." She made sure I had more than enough food to carry home with us. Often, we may not realize how little things can mean so much to someone else. I was having thoughts of dying and thoughts of leaving my family. How could I possibly think about what we would eat today or tomorrow? In fact, if it had not been for her meals, we would not have had any food to eat. She took the heaviness of that burden away. She prepared dinner every day and a special Sunday dinner, as she usually did for her family; she added two more permanent plate settings for us in her home. Each ingredient and every recipe she prepared revealed her love for God's people. She and I spent time together talking about life and how she found herself in Georgia by way of Virginia. Without family, just as I had been, her love for family was not biased or selfish. She opened her home and family up to me and made me feel just as important as her entire family. God knew just who He could use; He knew what I needed to help me get through to the other side, for my family had always been my support. I dedicate my story to my mom Viola and Claretha, my Wounded Healers.

One day while lying in my prayer closet, I heard a doorbell ring. It wasn't my doorbell, and there was no way I could be hearing the bell from my neighbor's home. It wasn't until I heard a soft yet straightforward voice says, "What are you expecting?" I knew it was God, and He knew my fear. I thought if I didn't say the word "die" out loud, I would not die. Yet, I felt as though I was dying. What I realized was my thoughts were not aligning with God's promises. His thoughts were higher than mine, and He has another plan. From that day forward, I walked in expectation of God's promises, that His mercy and grace would find me, and that healing was my portion, and no weapon formed against me shall prosper. The thyroid cancer journey may have left me with a sunken scar in my throat, but the scar represents the journey I had gone through. It would be a reminder of the request I had made to God; to use me so my family, my daughter, or her children, and children's children would be set free from cancer. I would be the vessel that God would use to break the curse.

Message to the readers: I want to remind every reader of this book and my story that God knows every battle and every obstacle you will come up against; you are not alone. He has armed you with the strength to be victorious. For our "trials are the purifying of our faith, it is being tested as fire tests and purifies gold" (1Peter 1:3). Be confident and know that the "trial and proving of your faith bring out endurance and steadfastness and patience" (James 1:3). Walk-in Faith!

Jacqueline Muhammad

Jacqueline Muhammad is known for her diligent work, dedication, and personal sacrifice to the human family's upliftment. She has been a proud member of the Nation of Islam since 1989. Jacqueline previously served as Muslim Girls in Training (MGT) Captain, responsible for women and girls' training. She has taken this knowledge and love for women to start United for Girls, a nonprofit organization designed to meet women and girls where they are and assist them with tools to navigate life. She is the President and CEO of Village 19 Consultant Group, and in 2020 she launched the inaugural Operation Grace, an initiative that feeds 1000 women over ten days during Ramadan.

Sister Jacqueline (as she is affectionately known) graduated Magna Cum Laude with a Bachelor of Arts degree in Communications. She has received several honors over the years, but the most important honor for her, however, is being God's daughter. Jacqueline currently works as a Senior Manager of Government & Customer Relations and is a Cleveland native. She is married to Student Minister Emeritus Roland Muhammad, and they are blessed with four children and six grandchildren.

To contact Sister Jacqueline, email unitedforgirls1@gmail.com.

WITHOUT PRESSURE THERE IS NO DIAMOND

Jacqueline Muhammad

"Bismillah." As a young adult, I did not know or understand the real need for a sisterhood, even though God blessed me with five biological sisters. Look at the word "sisterhood;" it can be defined as the ability to be loved unconditionally by a female (Sister) and one who can cover you using that love as the foundation (hood). I thank Allah (God) for the Sisterhood of the Nation of Islam and the mighty Muslim Girls in Training (MGT) class – it was there that I learned what Sisterhood is and what my role should be as I relate to an intimate group of sister-friends as well as the broader family of "sisters."

One of the many examples of Sisterhood in my life goes like this...

After giving birth to our last child in 2002, my husband and I were happy and excited to bring our son home from the hospital. We were looking forward to introducing him to his siblings and extended family members. At the time, we had a fourteen-year-old and a two-and-a-half-year-old at home; our adult daughter was away at school. Never did I imagine I would have the thought of harming one of my children. But it happened, and at that moment, I learned that postpartum depression is real. I also learned that Allah (God) is still present and once again loves me even in the midst of pain and pressure.

Because I am a planner, I thought I prepared everything before going to the hospital. The house was clean, the baby's room was decorated beautifully, and all supplies were ready to go. All I needed to do was count the days until I would bring this new addition to our family home. During this pregnancy, I would pray all the time, asking God to touch my womb and make my baby healthy and strong physically. However, my most important prayer was asking him to bless my baby to be his reflection on the world. I stayed there in prayer, moment by moment, day after day. Spiritually, I thought I was also ready.

Then the day came, I gave birth to a healthy baby boy, and we were headed home, ready to introduce him to his siblings. The next week would be the most challenging for me as a mother. I, of course, intended to nurse my new baby, but he would not latch on well. I struggled every day. On one particular day (I remember it so vividly as if it were yesterday). Instead of gaining weight, my baby was losing weight. I was so frustrated because I didn't want to be a failure. I didn't want to be defeated. You see, many times, I had coached other sisters to fight through the negativity, internally and externally, that would come up to suggest reasons to quit trying to nurse and just to give the baby a bottle of cow's milk. I continued to try; the pain was excruciating. And by the way, where was God when I needed him? On this day, my two-and-a-half-year-old asked for something to eat. I responded, "Okay, in a minute." But he kept going, asking over and over again, as children do. My 14-year-old was at school and my husband at work. At that moment, I needed a release from the pressure I was under. The physical mind took over and said, "The next time he asks, pick him up and throw him out that window - all the nagging will just go away." In the next moment, I began to cry – holding my screaming newborn, who just wanted to be nursed, and holding my two-and-a-half-year-old, who just wanted to eat. As I cried, I prayed; you know that sobbing kind of prayer - wailing and wailing, begging for help and mercy. This went on until what seemed like an instant later, my phone rang. It was Sister Joyce Muhammad, asking if I needed anything (I tear up now as I recall the story because at that moment, I was truly broken, and there she was). Initially, my strong "physical" will said to her, "No, I'm good." I thanked her for calling to check on me. God then spoke to me and said, "This is the answer to your prayer." Just like that, I was about to deny my blessing – about to allow the physical self to take over again; this false sense that I can make it through this moment without relying on others. I told Sister Joyce, "Yes, there is something I need. Can you possibly take my two-and-a-half-year-old for a couple of hours?" She said, "Yes, of course." In what seemed like a matter of minutes - she was there picking him up. Now that's "sisterhood" - that's "covering." By the time he returned several hours later, I had been successful in feeding my newborn. My fourteen-year-old and husband had returned home, and no one ever knew I had stepped into postpartum depression - albeit just for a few moments – it could have proven deadly.

Every sister thereafter that I learn of having a newborn with small children at home, I make it a point to take the older child(ren) out for a while. I live by the motto, "To whom much is given, much is required." By the grace of Allah (God), I am here with all of my children so that I may share with you my encounter with both God and Satan. Now, let me be clear, this encounter was not external; it was definitely an internal experience. And in my moment of pain and pressure, Sister Joyce was my blessing. Just think about how God was aligning things all at the same time. Was it my fervent prayer that did it? I tend to think so, but all I knew is that I had a need. SHE was the sister I needed at that moment. She had to be obedient to the voice within her to call me, not knowing she was walking into my healing. She never knew she was assisting me in my faith journey. She never knew she was God's vessel to release the pressure I was under. She never knew she was my saving grace. She never knew she was helping me recognize how I had allowed Satan to creep into my reality. She never knew she was my reminder that God never left me nor forsook me. She never knew she was helping me in all these ways. She only knew there was a sister in need, and she was going to cover that sister - me. So, I thank Allah (God) for her love, for her covering, for her obedience, for her Sisterhood. Thank you, Sister Joyce, thank you.

Message to the Reader: Now, was I going to throw my son out the window? Probably not, but to entertain it – to have the thought come up within me in the first place was so disturbing. Had God's daughter allowed the whispering of the slinking devil to take her off course? Yes. In that moment of pressure and frustration, I opened the door wide enough for Satan (in the form of negative thought) to come in. And that is how it happens. Satan lies and waits until "life happens," until we are confronted with stress, disappointment, or frustration, and then he shows himself directing us how to relieve the stress. This relief from Satan will forever be in the physical because Satan's job is not to draw us nearer to God but away from him. This is where study and prayer are so necessary. We must prepare for war in the time of peace. Life is good, but we continue to believe, to study the word of God, to pray, fast, and practice charity – (to put on the full armor of God), so that we will be ready to enter the battle with Satan and come out victorious by the grace of God, and in my case, with the help of a Sister.

If you are experiencing postpartum depression or feel like Satan is whispering in your ear, know that you are not alone. To be vulnerable before God is the beginning of healing and to get the help we need in a moment of pressure and pain. The other side of the bridge is just a prayer away.

When prayer becomes our habit,
miracles become our lifestyle.
– Student Minister Nuri Muhammad

CONTRIBUTING WRITERS

Dr. Jill Barry

Dr. Jill Barry, also known as "Dr. B," was born and raised in Michigan, completing medical school at Michigan State University College of Human Medicine in 1989. She came to Cleveland, Ohio, to complete her Internal Medicine Residency at St. Luke's Hospital. Then she joined Dr. Mona Reed (now Faith Medical Associates, Inc.) in private practice specializing in Internal Medicine (diabetes, hypertension, arthritis, acid reflux, etc.) with a Vascular Medicine focus. She takes time with her patients and believes that medicine and faith work together. She has provided non-traditional education by writing articles under the heading "Ask Dr. B" in Horizon Magazine.

To contact Dr. Barry, email faith_medicalassoc@yahoo.com

IN THE ARMS OF MY GRANDMA

Dr. Jill Barry

A few decades back, I had a spat with my family, none of whom lived near me. It was all a matter of principle. At the time, I didn't know what else to do since the issue was really important to me. I tried to explain my perspective about their reaction to a situation. They seemed indifferent; we were at an impasse. It wasn't that I didn't love them. I just thought that time would bring understanding. You know - that means they would figure out that they were wrong and I was right, and then there would be a resolution. (That's supposed to be funny, except it's true.) You might think to yourself; how does anyone end up in a situation like that? Well, don't ask because you might just learn.

We didn't talk for years, except I communicated with my mom. She was ill at the time. I remember praying that she would be okay through it all. For years nothing changed. Then one day, I received a note from a member of my family. It was a "just to let you know" kind of note. Included in the message was a copy of my mom's obituary. Time stopped. I lost all the breath in my lungs. When my breath came back, I lost it again. My life changed forever. I just never believed that would happen. My mom was gone! I would never see her again. I would never be able to tell her I loved her again. I would never be able to say how sorry I was that I wasn't there. I would never be able to explain.... How could my family let that happen? How could God let that happen? There are no words in the English language to describe all the things that I felt. Most of all, I felt the loss, the unreconcilable loss. Standing up for the principal, my issue, cost me so much. How could I move forward from that? How did I let it happen? How could I look at any family without being swarmed by emotions? How could I celebrate anything? Days and years passed by, and I got really good at just taking steps. In my mind and heart, I was waiting for God to show me how to deal with the circumstances and my emotions. No, that's not it. I was waiting for God to heal my emotions. At some point, I started to notice that I wanted to see my Grandma, my mom's mom. So, what was so hard about that? Well, she lived in the same city as my family. Going to see her meant going to the place I last saw my mom. Yet, that desire to see Grandma grew stronger and stronger. I got some prodding from friends who would ask me if I had talked to any members of my family. My Pastor would give me a Word about particular relatives. Finally, I decided to make the trip. I called the facility where she lived to make sure she would be there and available.

The drive that took several hours was a blur. I remember parking, walking in, and being directed to her room. And there she sat, my nearly 100-year- old beloved Grandma. Despite her advancing Alzheimer's Dementia, we talked. It's amazing to me how we talked. We went out to lunch and had a beautiful time. There was just one more thing I needed to do before leaving. I had to go to the cemetery. I asked Grandma if she would go with me, and of course, she said yes. You see, I felt that I needed her to go with me because I was too wounded to go alone. With Grandma at my side, we went to the cemetery. Walking into the mausoleum was probably one of the hardest things I've ever done, but it was necessary for me. I sat there with Grandma. We held hands, hugged, and sobbed. We consoled each other.

In that mausoleum, with Grandma, my path to healing began. I doubt my Grandma had a clue what she did for me that day or the several times we returned. It's like she was there just for me, to guide me through. She was the strength I needed. I'm so thankful for Grandma. What would I have done without her? I'm so glad I didn't have to find out.

Nowadays, every once in a while, I have an opportunity to counsel a family whose loved one is nearing the end of life. I like to remind them; you won't get these moments back.

It is never too late to listen to what the Lord puts in your heart.

Minister Vanessa Davis

The importance is in your relationships! This simple but essential life truth has been a cornerstone of Vanessa Davis since she was a child growing up in Cleveland, Ohio.

She is now a wife and mother of three adult sons. Vanessa is a successful business owner, spiritual coach, youth and parent educator.

Vanessa founded a nonprofit organization "Deborah's Place." For eight years in the greater Cleveland area, she trained, coached, encouraged, and provided teen mothers resources from all walks of life. Vanessa Davis has been passionate about teaching parents how to coexist with others without toxic behavior to benefit a child.

Vanessa is currently an educator of autistic high schoolers at a Christian Academy. She is the co-owner of "Up-N-Down Cleaning," a commercial cleaning business outside Tampa, FL, with her husband of 30 years.

PURPOSEFUL PAIN

Minister Vanessa Davis

Growing up in somewhat of a stable home with dad and mom, which was not common in my family or generation, my siblings and I did not understand or even know the dysfunction we lived in. My dad went to work every day, and my mom was a stay-at-home mom. Some would probably say this was the ideal family, at least I thought so. Being the oldest child of three (now five), I was very observant of what was happening. Some might say I was noisy, maybe I was, but I wanted to know why certain things were happening, like the bullet hole in our living room after returning home late from grandma's house. I wanted to know why dad was not at home, and little did I know I wouldn't see him again for three years.

Dad was our security, and he made sure we did not lack anything, and mom was the best. She made sure we were always clean, fed, and healthy. I would have never imagined that my life would never be the same on that Friday night. We no longer had a safe place, and as time went on, we no longer had a home. We had to move to grandma's house, where there was no stability, and the dysfunction was real. We eventually moved out. We had to move back to grandma's house a second time, and this is where the dysfunction truly began in my life. We had no structure or order, and everyone was pretty much on their own to make sure they had what they needed.

I grew up faster than I wanted to. Mom was now a single mother with three children, no money, no direction, and we struggled tremendously. We were going from a home where we had everything we needed to a place where we didn't have anything. As the eldest, I felt like I had to help my mother. I didn't know what to do; it was always dad's job to make sure we were okay. To help feed my brother and sister, we would get pop bottles and turn them in for money, and in the summer, we had a lemonade stand. It was four years later that I would see my dad again.

We moved from my grandma's house, and my life was never the same after our move to 80th and Wade Park; this was my place of darkness. I was twelve years old when we moved to an unfamiliar area; this was the first time my mom, siblings, and I lived by ourselves. I remember sitting on the porch, getting used to the neighborhood. Little did I know someone was watching me. I will say I was the prey for this predator. I am not sure how long he was watching me, but he eventually made his way across the street and then into our home. He watched us long enough to know that my mom was a single mother. He started dating my mother, and soon he moved in not long after they started dating. The man we knew nothing about molested and abused me for four years of my life, which caused so much pain, bitterness, and anger. During this, there were other emotional tragedies, like promiscuity and drinking as a teenager, which led to getting pregnant at the age of eighteen. The abuse and emotional tragedies were very painful. All of it made it challenging for me to have healthy relationships.

I held on to that pain for years. I met my now-husband, who I could not be the wife he deserved and that God intended because I didn't know God. I didn't know how to be a godly wife because I never saw it. I held on to the pain and hurt from my past for many years. I needed healing from this hurt. I knew something was missing in my life, but I didn't know what that something was. I couldn't be a wife the way I desired; I had too much unforgiveness in my heart. I am so grateful God used my best friend (since 3rd grade) to lead me to the Lord. This woman of God was so instrumental in me accepting Jesus as my Savior. Lounette and I were inseparable as teenagers. We began going to church at the age of twelve. We grew up, and Lounette married her high school sweetheart and eventually became the church's First Lady. Lounette passed away in April 2017. I was not surprised by the number of attendees at her service; many spoke on how she led them to Christ. I will never forget how God used her to help me begin my healing process. She never gave up on me, and because of that, I was able to forgive the man who stole my childhood and have a godly marriage of thirty years.

I was able to turn my pain into purpose. I formed a non-profit parenting program, Deborah's Place of Refuge, to help single moms know their value and self-worth. Debs Place (as it is affectionately called) was designed to help single moms' complete high school and move on to higher education. Each mom had to complete her training, education, budgeting, and parenting classes. Debs Place also had community partners who managed low-income housing to help house our families. We would pay the first month's rent, security deposit and furnish the apartment if needed. We helped over 60 young mothers, and many of them have great success stories.

Message to the readers: I hope this story will bless and encourage you to become the best you God created you to be; your pain is truly purposeful.

And the God of all grace, who called you to his eternal glory in Christ, after you have suffered a little while, will himself restore you and make you strong, firm and steadfast. 1 Peter 5:10

LaVerne Dawson

LaVerne Dawson is the First Lady at Grace Tabernacle, located in Lyndhurst, Ohio. She serves on the Usher Board, is involved in Christian Education and Sunday School. She is a retired Cosmetologist of 37 years. She is a graduate of East High School and Vogue Beauty Academy. She obtained her Manager's and Instructor's license, along with many other certificates over many years in the beauty industry. LaVerne is the loving wife of Pastor Wayne Dawson of Grace Tabernacle and a Newscaster of Fox 8. She's the mother of Danielle, three adult children Tamara, Crystal, Tyshin, and grandmother of eight. Laverne has a heart for women and desires to see them become whole in Christ.

SISTAH-HOOD

LaVerne Dawson

At the age of 22, I had returned home after moving back from Los Angeles, California, the trip of a lifetime. Hollywood is known for its glitz and glamour, a dream world that is exciting and attractive. Nevertheless, it is also the reality of many shattered dreams. But like the great Maya Angelou wrote, "Up from the past that's rooted in pain, I rise." In Tupac Shakur's lyrics, "Now let me welcome everybody to the wild, wild west." I would like to simply title this story "Sistah-Hood" because I'm about to introduce you to some real, true sistahs from the Diamond State of Delaware, the Lone Star State of Texas, and the State known as Georgia Peach. Each migrated to the State of California and worked overtime just to make a living in the City of Los Angeles. True sisterhood helps us to share both the light and the dark parts of our life journeys. It allows us to see who we are in the eyes of another woman. That validation and affirmation are what make this story powerful, meaningful, and unforgettable.

In the words of Gladys Knight's recording of "You're The Best Thing That Ever Happened to Me," I often thought, if anyone should ever write my life story for whatever reason there might be, my story could not be told without Jasmine, Niecy, and Bernadette. They were "Hood Angels" that God sent to care for me. They were outcasts looked upon as hood-rats. The slang term "hood-rat" means being low class, sexually promiscuous, and with little to no morals or self-respect. Many times, in the inner- city, better known as "The Hood," you are mischaracterized; but thankfully, we know our destiny is not defined by what others think or say about us. In fact, God often uses the downtrodden, the oppressed, and those who are mistreated and talked about, like Mary Magdalene and the harlot known as Rehab. God is known to turn ashes into beauty so others may see His glory.

What I found intriguing was the bond these three Sistahs shared with one another. They didn't lose heart, although they were broken, battered, wounded, and considered damaged goods; no longer desirable or valuable according to populace standards. What they had was one another, and they made a pact to have one another's back. Together they felt secure, protected, and safe. Then here comes a misfit wandering in the wilderness, lost and alone, desperately trying to find her way home. The funny thing is, how did this little square, one hundred pounds, a 20-year-old young woman raised in the church with two loving parents, the fourth of seven siblings, end up here?

We were poor but not impoverished. We had a nice house, nice clothes and plenty to eat. We were a family well-respected in the neighborhood. How did she wind up here? How could such different lifestyles so mysteriously come together? I often kid around and say, being the middle child, I got lost in the sauce. Now, if you were to ask me what is "lost in the sauce" really means, well, I really don't know. But I often felt overlooked, being that middle child, and I wanted to find my own way.

Famous last words. So off to California, I went. I had big dreams, little money, and no plans. So you can see where this story is headed. But that's enough about me. Let's get back to my "Guardian Angels" - the three bad girls, Jasmine, Niecy, and Bernadette, whom Donna Summers made a song about in the early eighties. You may remember the song lyrics, "Toot toot, hey, beep beep...see them out on the streets at night, picking up all kinds of strangers if the price is right." Yes, that was Jasmine, Niecy, and Bernadette - bad girls and bad girls are not usually celebrated or praised, but I will never forget how they provided me shelter, food, and a sound direction without hesitation or expectation. God said, "I'll never leave you or forsake you." It was by the hearts and hands of those who society rejected that took me in and nourished me back to health. It's been 40 years, and I often think of them and where they may be today. I pray that the Lord has blessed them as He has blessed me down through the years. They were God-sent. I've never thought in a million years I would be asked to share my life's ups and downs. Truly in my early years, God was there between each line of pain and glory. Jasmine, Niecy, and Bernadette, you will always be my unsung heroes.

Clarissa Foster

Clarissa Foster attended Jane Addams Business Careers Center where she studied to become a Legal Secretary. Clarissa pursued and earned her Bachelor of Science Degree in Paralegal Studies from Myers College. Clarissa received her Master's Degree in Business Administration from Myers University.

At the age of 30, Clarissa became the youngest black female CEO in the State of Ohio to own and operate an escrow and title insurance agency. She is also the Managing Member of National Paralegal Services, LLC, a full- service legal document preparation service. She's the People's Paralegal.

Clarissa is a contributing author of "Permission to Speak," a compilation of writings sponsored by the City of Cleveland, and a co-author of "Diary of a Ready Woman." Distinguished honors include the A.B. Bonds Award from Baldwin Wallace College (University), The TRIO Achievers Award by The Ohio Association of Educational Opportunity Program Personnel (OAEOPP), Community Leader Recognition Award from the City of Cleveland Mayor Frank G. Jackson, and the Prosperous Young Black Women Award. Clarissa is a proud member of Positive Plus. She is also a proud mother of one adult son and a grandmother.

To contact Clarissa email, NationalParalegalServices@gmail.com or visit her website: NationalParalegalServices.com

BLOOM WHERE YOU ARE PLANTED

Clarissa Foster

TRAGIC NEW YEAR 2020

I remember thinking on New Year's Eve how the year 2020 was going to be BIG! I had so many plans. My thoughts were so grand that I can remember sitting there smiling to myself at the prospects to come.

On the evening of January 1, we all joined my parents at their home for a king crab dinner fest and New Year celebratory dinner. Everything was wonderful! My mom did her usual running around, tending to the family. My dad sat in his comfortable chair. We all just had a great time together. As the evening grew late, we prepared to say our goodbyes. Who knew that would be the last time we would tell each other, "I love you." The next morning, my dad, Rev. Willie M. Simpson, would die of a heart attack. The best dad I had ever known was gone! This would be the start of the worst year of my life!

IT'S ALL ABOUT MOM

Life as we knew it was forever changed! I was sticking to my mother like glue! We were already close. If you saw her, you saw me; but now we were pretty much inseparable. She would often tell me she was fine, but I didn't hear any of it. If I had my way, she would move in with me or me with her. We all missed my dad terribly and were grieving. It was hard. Mom missed him a lot. She was always looking at his obituary. There were copies all around the house, even in her bed. She would often quote him or recite stories they had. Then she would drift off into her thoughts. They were husband and wife and also great friends.

Mom said now she is going to start doing what she has always wanted to do. She was trying to be strong, especially in front of the family. She wanted to travel to Guadalupe, learn Spanish, and most importantly, get her foundation GITGP – God Is the Greatest Power Foundation – started. She was very excited about this foundation because it focused on helping grandparents who raise their grandchildren. My mom lived for children. Sadly, my mom didn't get a chance to fulfill her wishes. On April 4, 2020, just three months after my dad passed, my mother, Mrs. Bettie Lou Simpson, passed away from heart disease.

EVERYTHING WENT DARK

I was completely devastated! Is there a word stronger than devastated? Did my very best friend, mother, confidant, security blanket, and everything I have in this world just die? Part of me wanted to go with her. I watched the paramedics work very hard to resuscitate her. I will NEVER forget those imagines.

Life as I knew it was over. Every day I cried and struggled to get up. Every day I struggled to shower, put on makeup, comb my hair, or smile. Every day felt like I had to act normal or people would not know how to behave around me. In reality, I was an emotional wreck inside. Me, the extravert - the one everyone else calls. I didn't know what to do. In times of trouble, no matter how deep or shallow, I would call my mother. Who do I call now? She was my person to call!!! I JUST WANTED TO SHOUT OUT LOUD ---UUUUUUUUGH WHHHHHYYYYY?!!!!

I can't close out this chapter without mentioning the planning of a proper funeral, amidst a pandemic, unlike anything we have ever seen in our lifetime. Spring and summer 2020 were the eye of the storm for COVID-19, and we were very limited in the number of people allowed for the viewing and funeral service. Personally, I believe my mom deserved a funeral fit for a queen.

Many people lost their lives to this disease. My mom was very careful concerning this pandemic; she would not even get out of the car to hug any of us. She would just wave. So, I respected the service and how it had to be handled because I knew she would certainly want everyone to err on the side of caution rather than take the risk of contracting the disease just to be there. We were allowed to stream the service live on Facebook for our family and friends to pay their respects to our beloved mom.

THE GENESIS OF HEALING

But as I sit here and write, I would be remiss if I didn't focus on my mother's many teachings. She, in all her wisdom, had prepared me for a time such as this. I was just so sad that I could not see. She often talked about her grandmother, Ella Brantley, who raised her until 12 years old. She was 81. Her mother, Ernestine Brantley Brown, passed away at the age of 23 when my mom was only three years old, and her sister was one year old. My mom spoke of not having her mother, but how grateful she was that God allowed her to not only raise her own children but be here to see and play pivotal roles in her grand and great-grand children's lives. There are so many stories and not enough room to articulate them. My mom was known for saying, no matter what is happening in your life or where you are in your life, "Bloom where you are planted." So, mom, I'm going to take your advice again and bloom where I am planted. I am yet on fresh uncharted grounds, but I'm sure your words will hold true as they always have. Thank you, mom!

As a family, we are so proud and honored that our wonderful and loving parents' legacy is humbly recognized in Ghana, West Africa. A beautiful Praying Sanctuary has been erected in honor of Reverend Willie M. Simpson to signify his decades of service as a Reverend and Pastor for the glory of God. Additionally, a Giving Kitchen named after my mother has been erected and will remain fully stocked, paying homage to the great Mrs. Bettie Lou Simpson, whose favorite place to be was her kitchen!

God is the Greatest Power!
– Bettie L. Simpson

Faith is the strength by which a shattered world shall emerge into the light.

– Hellen Keller

Linda Gamble

Linda Gamble is a retired Administrative Assistant and Program Coordinator from associate institutions within the Catholic Diocese of Cleveland. She was educated in the private, public, and continuing education systems of Cleveland, Ohio. Linda is highly experienced in non-traditional program development. Under her tutelage, countless youth have benefited from her establishment of training and employment opportunities, mentoring, and enrichment initiatives designed to give them a deeper appreciation of community, education, and life as they enter adulthood.

Linda has a heart for those in need. Many have been fed through her community meals. She began at her worship facility in 2014 until 2018 and has warmed stomachs at the local men's homeless shelter since 2017.

To contact Linda email, lmggamble@sbcglobal.net

ONE WOMAN

Linda Gamble

When an invitation came to tell of my wounded healer, I immediately began to seek a person who directed me through a terrible life situation. A wound? My thought was that, by the grace of God, there had been no tragedy or trauma throughout my life. My injuries were not traumatizing or tragic. "Tragic" is not how I would describe my story. I was not on drugs or physically abused. I have not been homeless or living on the streets. Nor have I lost a family member to violence or a child to an unfortunate situation or illness. Did I have deep-seated challenges? Yes. But they only seemed "tragic" to me, in that they were of the heart, buried so deep inside that it seemed impossible to reach them. No band-aid could cover them.

My challenges were my children - four daughters and a son. My eldest, Lawna, smart as a whip (an old saying for someone who has a great mind); Daena, my second born - loving, caring, and a pleaser; Carla - friendly, competitive, and rambunctious; George - a happy and spoiled Mama's boy; and Erin - a quiet perfectionist adopted after my marriage separation. I remember praying to be a good mother, not just a woman with a child (ren). Motherhood was not easy for me. I birthed two children before marriage and experienced a failed marriage with four children. How was I going to survive? Only God knew. I was wounded. Each stage in life one doesn't excel in or conquer is a wound. There is a healer (or healers) along the way you don't think of as healers. A teacher, sponsor, friend, neighbor, or family member can be your healer. Many women throughout your life are healers. Open your heart; listen, and endure the atmosphere that comes with her presence. The environment that surrounds a woman speaks to her likes, dislikes, or desires. I want to be like… Not me… I don't like what was said… An atmosphere or gathering speaks to power, whether negative or positive. I decided which power I wanted to receive. Either of them can be reached without words but through a feeling.

ONE HEALER

During my marriage, we lost our home because of irresponsible behavior concerning our finances. We were a family of five with nowhere to go. A friend from my church named Martha offered to take us in until we could recover. Imagine the feeling of having a family, and you are unable to provide housing. You're devastated and lost in hopelessness. To say the least, her family of six and my family of five were living under one roof, adults under another's rule. Martha taught me about love, finance, proper discipline, and God. I knew about God but did not really know Him or have a deep relationship with Him. I learned things of prayer, worship, and surrendering myself to God. What I learned has taken me through so many of the challenges throughout my adulthood that would come later; an unfaithful husband, being on welfare, and other frustrations.

SECOND HEALER

Now, with my second child from my marriage, additional income was needed in the family. I don't know whether what was in my heart was showing on my face or if someone was actually reading my mind. Thus, began an answered prayer of "being a good mother." No, not in the sense of birthing a child, but love for many children. Lydia Harris, the Principal at St. Adalbert Catholic School, inquired if I had an interest in working part-time. Mrs. Harris took me under her wing and taught me how to meet the needs of young people. She walked with me from becoming a school aide to a typing instructor during the computer age onset to teach. Mrs. Harris' motto was, "The care you give is the love you receive in return, and there isn't a child that cannot be taught." Mrs. Harris was instrumental in my son attending an eight-week summer program in Washington, D.C. that addressed the culture, spirituality, and growth of young Black children. Neither of us knew then, but we hoped this program would help my son through years to come. Mrs. Harris encouraged what later became the beginning of a 30-year journey of youth programs.

HEALERS ALONG THE WAY

Sr. Claire Sharpshair, who recognized something in me that could turn the minds of young people began to help heal wounds that still bring tears. However, they now are love tears knowing I made a difference in many young lives. Mary Russell made ideas come to life. She never questioned, just asked questions - questions to process the thought of an idea. They were ideas and causes she also thought supported and would lead to better financial lives. Mary has been a foundation of caring, sharing, and building up lives as she giggles and says, "Great! I trust you". Lawna Gamble, my daughter, has been listening, walking, and sorting through the wounds that threaten to hold me back in this thing called life.

Pastor Sharina George

Pastor Sharina George has served in ministry for over seventeen years. She is called "mini-dynamo" by many for her bold and unapologetic delivery of the Word of God. She is truly a student and lover of the Word of God. She has a genuine love for people and truly believes, "One word can change everything!" She is also Founder and Chief Editor of Authentic Magazine and Owner of Xcellence Marketing. She is the author of Destiny by Design (2012) and Broken by Design (2017). She is a psalmist and songwriter with a passion for authentic praise and worship.

To contact Pastor Sharina email, sharinageorge@gmail.com

A RARE ROSE

Pastor Sharina George

My garden was beautiful and pure. There were vibrant colors, a fresh breeze, and plenty of lands to grow upon. It was youthful and free, untainted by the pollution life has to offer. My garden was innocent and optimistic about growing into the rose God made her be, when one day an ill wind comes along and takes away the fragrance of my rose. He took things I did not choose to give him. He plucked up my garden and trampled the petals under his feet, with no thought of how this would affect my tomorrow.

What is a garden to do when something so precious is stolen? After all, the garden is made of the look, the smell, and the poise of its beauty. Even though the garden had been bruised, it was so mentally disturbed that, instead of running in the opposite direction of the ill wind, she runs into more thieves that would take a rose each time she encountered them.

The garden grew dark and cold; her life almost gone, no breeze or sun could be found. Lonely and depressed was the state of my garden. Who would come along and help me to grow and flourish again? Who would be my rescue in the middle of a directionless ocean? The darkness was so thick that the garden tried to pluck up the last few signs of life. With no one to talk to, and it seems no one understands, what is a garden to do?

In the distance, a beautiful woman named Michelle had been prepared by God for the tedious task of rebuilding this worn-down garden. She took me into her bosom and allowed peace to be my healer and sustainer. She wrapped me in clothes of love and fed me with God's word. She nursed me back to strength as my Creator was giving me my reason why, the reason why God created the garden, allowed it to be trampled, and was building it back up again. I found me and why she was connected to this Rare Rose named Michelle. Her life's roots intertwined with mine like the roots of a tree wrapped around a rock. Like a tree that is planted by the water, I began to soak in her deep roots that allowed me to heal. Her love was seen for me and my little rose (my daughter). Her wisdom was very gentle and allowed me to grow along my life's path. She did not force my growth but simply allowed me to be led by her gracious example lived out in front of me.

This woman soared in like an eagle and caused me to experience growth in places that were once dead, places I thought could never live again. She caused me to think more of myself than what the thief tried to define me to be. She took off the other layers of her petals and wrapped me in them until I was healed, healthy, and whole. She introduced me to the Lover of my soul, the only One who could truly repair my garden. Michelle Robinson was my God-sent foster mother who also became my lifesaver. Today I take the time to honor her for loving me back to life.

Trouble finding God? Lose yourself!

The pain you feel today will be the strength you will feel tomorrow.

(no author)

Laquania Graham

Under the auspices of Sheree's Mirror Project, LLC, Laquania Graham has been blessed to commence a host of initiatives designed to spread the significance of education, healing, as well as virginity and abstinence until marriage. God's grace has propelled Laquania onto unfathomable platforms as she endeavored to leave her audiences with hope and a will to persevere.

Laquania is a graduate of Cuyahoga Community College and hails both a Bachelor's and Master's degree from Cleveland State University. She is also a playwright and author of What Are You Bringing to the Table? Her fifth book, The Abstinence Bible, will launch in 2021.

LET GOD USE YOUR HANDS

Laquania Graham

Being at home was a reminder that I didn't have anything beyond condiments in my refrigerator. It was a reminder that I looked good on the outside, but I was suffering inside. I felt like a failure, embarrassed that I had not progressed in various areas of my life that would have lessened the chance of my circumstance. I had three college degrees, published three books, and owned my home. Yet, after paying my tithes and bills, my bank account was still negative $14-$22 every two weeks if I didn't omit something.

It was Valentine's Day, and I was single, without children or a roommate, so my home environment could only be what I had created. Nevertheless, I wanted to be as far away as possible. I stalled by driving around before forcing myself to go home and ultimately face the inevitable. I unlocked the door and sat down at the kitchen table to see what I could conjure up in terms of a meal. I checked the mail and saw a Valentine's Day card from my mom. Unbeknownst to my financial challenges, she had also enclosed $40 in the card. Well, that $40 may as well have been $4 million! I quickly put my shoes back on and rushed to the grocery store on two wheels. God had sent help, and I had money to buy food! It was all I could do to keep from trembling with tears and gratitude to arrive at the store safely.

I can recall another instance where I had just gotten approval for someone to edit my fourth book. I could barely contain my excitement, even though I needed at least $1,500 to get my project off the ground. I met up with my friend, Taylor, and spewed all kinds of potential fundraising ideas, which I knew sounded like a speeding train of words. She did her best to grasp my plan but ultimately cut me off to inform me that she would gift me $1,000 immediately. Once again, I was trembling, confused by how fast God had wiped away the anxiety and spoke peace to a storm brewing in my mind. If there was ever a doubt about Him approving of my new book, it was quickly erased. I didn't even know my friend had that kind of disposable income, let alone for her to sow into a book she would never read. If those examples weren't enough to prove God had not forgotten about me, I could remember not having enough money for lunch via the vending machine that day. My coworker, Ailene, called to let me know she somehow got more food than what she had ordered and asked if I wanted her extra. Tears welled up in my eyes because God had set it up so that her extra would be my blessing. As much as I wanted to run thru the halls towards the promised food, I gave myself a pep talk about not seeming so anxious, lest she finds out how hungry I really was. I don't think I was successful in my efforts to be as nonchalant as possible because there were a few subsequent occasions that she continued to accidentally get "extra." Each time, it was as if God was hugging and loving me through her.

I refused to compromise my purity to receive financial assistance and encouraged other women to do the same. God was trying to teach me how to rely on Him and not on my job, but I didn't want to believe I hadn't failed in some way. I applied for part-time jobs that never called me back, all while looking for a change in my pockets, under-car rugs, and in my piggy bank in order to have lunch or dinner. God being God, I orchestrated help through these women (and others) while I was doing my best to keep my head above water throughout a very humbling season.

Now that my debt to income ratio has changed, I enjoy being a blessing into the unsuspecting lives of others. I make it my business to sow into at least one person every two weeks. From cooking for the downtrodden to supporting t-shirt businesses or a book launch,

I've begun to favor the beauty of "just because" gifts. I keep a picture of my once-empty refrigerator close by to remind me that God wants to use my hands. I had to come out of self-pity and believe that God hadn't forsaken me in my valley experience. Trials didn't mean I wasn't loved.

A stranger or someone you know is wounded and facing a battle right now. There is something you can do. Let God use your hands.

Jeanette Griffin

Jeanette was born in Alliance, Ohio, in 1972 to her parents, Johnny Triplett and Paulette (Babb) Triplett. At the age of two, Jeanette, her parents, and two older sisters moved to Canton, Ohio, where she resided until getting married on June 15, 1996, to Blaine A. Griffin. Blaine and Jeanette moved to Cleveland with their oldest son, Royce. By 1999, Jeanette had another son, Rajon, and was pregnant with Blaine, Jr., who was born in October 1999. This was also the year the young family moved into their home on Larchmere Ave. Currently, Jeanette works for the Central Collection Agency. She and her husband are approaching their 25th wedding anniversary and are proud to have raised three amazing sons.

MORE THAN A NEIGHBOR

Jeanette Griffin

Being a young wife and mother is not as easy as people make it seem. Being a twenty-three-year-old and moving to a new city without the family support that I was used to was difficult. A few good people crossed my path before moving on Larchmere, where my village began to form. The very first person I met was Mrs. Joyce Pratt. She took me under her wing and became like a second mom to me. We would sit on her porch for hours and talk about things I was going through, being the young wife of a very ambitious husband with great potential and three little boys watching our every move.

One of the greatest things Mrs. Pratt told me was not to lose myself in my husband and children. I had to know who I was outside of them. For many years I felt like I was only Blaine's wife and Royce, Rajon, and Blaine, Jr.'s mom. I had no life that didn't center around the four men in my household, which was not healthy for any of us. Hearing some of the things Joyce went through when she was younger let me know that I wasn't the first woman to go through the things I was going through, and I wouldn't be the last. It also gave me another reason to keep my head up and continue fighting for my family.

There was never a moment that Mrs. Pratt would ever sugar coat things for me. She was always a straight shooter and would let me know when I was wrong. She never looked at me any different, and everything I did was because it was my choice and not her influence. Joyce had a way of helping me talk through the difficult things; the next thing I knew, I had figured my own problem out, with her just being a sounding board.

Something else that I try to live by is not running to my mom or sisters when we are having problems in the household. Joyce would say, you may be mad now, but eventually, that would change, and if you keep going to a family with all the negative things, they may look at Blaine differently. I never want my views to affect the individual relationship they have with my husband because I know I'm not going anywhere.

Thinking back to when I found out my mom had stage 4 lung cancer in 2009, I was a total wreck and felt horrible that I lived an hour away from her. Joyce helped me realize I wasn't a bad daughter because I couldn't be there with her every day. Because of Joyce, I was able to get over my guilt, be present with my mom, and still take care of my family all at the same time.

I'm so happy I could sit down with Mrs. Pratt to thank her for all the talks we had over the years. Joyce knew how much I genuinely appreciated and loved her while she was still here on this earth. I miss her more than most people, now that she has passed on. Most times, when I sit on my porch, I look two houses over and smile, thinking about all the years we spent there together talking, laughing, crying, and just enjoying each other. All I can do now is remember her and pass on the knowledge that she planted in me. It feels amazing to talk to young wives and mothers and help them realize they're not in this alone.

"And now these three remain, Faith, Hope & Love. But the greatest of these is Love"

1 Corinthians 13:13

Maggie Haas

Maggie Haas is a native of Cleveland, Ohio. She is a single mother who has raised two boys. In 2014, Maggie obtained her Real Estate license while continuing her work in the corporate world's financial sector. After the murder of her youngest son, Anthony, in May of 2018, she has fulfilled her dream and her son's wish to start her own business. Her company, ANT Professional Services, specializes in environmental hazard testing. She enjoys traveling and spending time with her friends and family, especially her son Aaron and Chris's, her bonus son.

LIFE AFTER LOSS

Maggie Haas

On May 10, 2018, my world shattered. Just three days before Mother's Day, my youngest son, Anthony Haas, was killed. I lost all sense of who I was, and I couldn't function. It was like living in a nightmare. Nothing is clear, but you can still see what's happening around you. It feels surreal. You are in a constant fog. When Anthony died, a piece of me died. Anyone who has lost a child knows exactly what that feeling is.

Anthony, my youngest son, was 23 when he was taken from us. He was still living at home. We had a very close bond, and Anthony protected me with the fierceness of a lion. He was my comedian and had a smile that would brighten any room. His charisma and personality were unmatched. Anyone who knew Anthony, instantly loved him. Losing Anthony sent me into a deep depression. I couldn't work, eat, sleep, or enjoy life anymore. I still have my oldest son and tried my best to push forward for him. But I was stuck. How was I supposed to live my life and carry on when half of me was gone?

One of my closest friends, Melissa, was the first to come to my house the morning after his death. She came bearing gifts that consisted of coffee and donuts in anticipation of all the people that arrived after her. Melissa has been by my side through all my trials and tribulations. She would often get Anthony when he was little and keep him for the weekend when my oldest son would go to his dad's house. She had no children at the time, so Anthony was like her first child. She saw me get sick from working at a company where I had black mold in my office. After eight years of employment, rather than allowing me to work from home, they let me go when doctors said I couldn't work in that environment anymore.

Melissa had quit her job in 2017 and started her own company.

Her company focuses on environmental hazard abatement. In the months following losing Anthony, she saw the toll that it had taken on me. She would often call or visit just to check on me and see if I needed anything. She hated seeing me sit in the house and do nothing. She knew that I had once wanted to start my own business. In February of 2019, she asked me to take a class with her on lead paint abatement. I kept giving her excuses as to why I couldn't do it. She kept reminding me that I needed to get up and get out of the house. She kept telling me that Anthony wouldn't want me to do that. I reluctantly went to the week-long class.

During the class, she knew exactly what to say to light that fire that I needed to start living again and stop just existing. She knew what Anthony had said to me when I had gotten sick from the mold. He said, "Mom, you are too smart to work for other people; you need to have your own business. I'm tired of seeing you work hard for other people, and they treat you like crap." She also talked about how the mold had affected me and how I could use this opportunity to help others. With her continuous support and words of encouragement that week, I decided that I was going to start my business. I told her I wanted to have a name that would be a tribute to Anthony. It was Melissa who knew how much pain I was in from losing Anthony. She knew how much it would mean to me to have something that would give Anthony's name a way to live on. She said the best way to honor him would be to officially start my company on the same date that he had died.

So, on May 10, 2019, ANT Professional Services was born. "Ant" was what we called Anthony. A cartoon version of Anthony is the company logo. Since my situation with the mold made Anthony say those words to me, I decided I wanted to do something with environmental hazards. I am currently a licensed Asbestos Hazard Evaluation Specialist and Lead Abatement Worker. Within the next year, I am planning on also becoming a licensed Lead Paint Hazard

Evaluation Specialist. With Melissa's words, support and push, I was able to get off the couch and use my pain as motivation to honor my son. I will use this business to honor Anthony's memory, fulfill his wishes for my life and live the dream I had before he was taken from us.

Message to the readers: The pain of losing a child never goes away. But what we do is learn how to cope and deal with the pain. The pain becomes a part of who we are. Use the pain as the motivation to continue to live in a manner that will honor our children and help others.

Lori Middleton-Haynes

Lori Middleton-Haynes had an extensive career as a Senior Account Executive at Imaginit Technologies. Her career in technology evolved from building long-term strategic relationships with top architects and engineers throughout the greater Cleveland area. Lori's passion for building a better community has taken her on a humanitarian work path. She has joined forces with the Gloria Pointer Teen Movement Foundation, helping to build dorms for children in Ghana, West Africa. In honor of her son, she has now built a dormitory for orphan boys; Willie Haynes, III Center of Love opened in January 2021. Her work in Ghana is just the beginning of a greater work God has set before her.

MY RIGHT AND MY LEFT ARMS

Lori Middleton-Haynes

As far back as I remember, I have had strong, loving, Black women at the center of my life. First and foremost, my mother, Constance R. Ledbetter (Middleton), made sure that God was the focal point of my life. Each of these women played a vital role in me becoming the woman that I am today. There came a time in my life when two of these ladies carried me when I could no longer carry myself. Jean Middleton and Brenda Tyson are my right and left arms. They have always held me up when I could not hold myself up. Growing up, I was always outgoing and optimistic, never letting things keep me down. However, there comes a time in life when the encumbrance of losing a loved one can cause a heavyweight to come upon you that only God can remove. It is the type of weight that had hit me several times in my life, like when my mother, Constance R. Ledbetter (Middleton), was called home to glory in March 2013.

My mother was a shining star in my eyes. She loved God and put Him first in her life. She also made sure that her children knew Him. She had so much love in her heart that a ray of light shined all over her. Her love came from God and overflowed to everyone that she encountered, especially her family. My mother carried the weight of her family in her heart, which at one point caused her more grief and heartache than she could have ever imagined. This type of grief came upon her and me in September 2000, from my sister-in-law's death and my eldest brother's imprisonment. Each of these scenarios broke her heart. These events burdened her so that they shattered her heart into pieces, causing her health to begin failing. We had to fight during this extremely trying period (with Jean leading the way) for visitation with our niece and nephews. It was crucial to the well-being of our mother, and we prevailed to a certain extent. We never gave up. I was devastated.

Due to these circumstances, I'd had an estranged relationship with my brother throughout his ten years in prison. I watched my family suffering, which caused me a great deal of heartache that manifested itself as anger and resentment toward my brother. During these years, my mother suffered two strokes, and though she was quite fragile in her body, she remained of sound mind, holding on to God's unchanging hand.

In late August of 2012, my father, Willie Ledbetter, had a fall and passed away suddenly, which was simply more than my mother's heart could bear. During these dark times, I found myself struggling. Although I pressed my way for my mom's sake, there were times when it felt as if I was crawling on my knees. It was times like these that Jean Middleton and Brenda Tyson held me up. After my father passed away, I moved in with my mother. My sister Jean and I took care of her while I was also taking care of my household. I can remember the conversation with Jean asking her, "What about mom's condition? What are we going to do?" Her response was one of confidence. She answered, "We are going to take care of mommy; however, she comes and whatever it takes. If she cannot walk, we will carry her. If she cannot talk, we will find a way to speak for her, and whatever she needs, we will provide." Jean smiled and told me, "She will be okay, Mook." Hearing my big sister's response gave me so much strength. I watched her take the lead, visiting my mom at the nursing homes and hospital, once and sometimes twice a day. While my family was going through all of this, Jean held up my mother, son, and me. She also carried her daughter, my brothers, our nieces and nephews, and my brother in prison.

During the summer of 2012, Jean took my mother to retirement parties, family gatherings, house warmings, and church services. Jean and I took my mother to see President Barak Obama's campaign event at Cleveland State University in the rain. These things may not seem important to someone else, but they gave hope to my mother. Though my mom's body was weak, her mind was strong as ever. My sister did not let the weight from all of this responsibility stop her, as she taught me to care for our mom and to do it with no fear; we rocked it together, and Brenda was right there holding us up and supporting our every step. Brenda has been here for us all of our lives - always right there whenever we need her.

A month before the dreadful day of my mother's passing, my brother was released from prison. When my mom saw him, she cried tears of joy. Within 30 days, my mom passed away. My relationship with my brother did not improve, but Jean found a way to protect us all from the explosive outburst that came whenever we were in the same room together. There was not much time for me to restore a relationship with him, as he passed away two years after my mom. Jean supported our brother without missing a beat while he was battling cancer and during his transition. She stood in the gap for me when I could not bear to help. Losing six family members in eight years (including Brenda's mom) was a strain on everyone, but it seemed to get the best of me. After my brother passed away, our family came together to begin our healing process.

In August 2020, the unthinkable happened. My only son died suddenly. Now I find myself on this familiar journey again. A journey that is almost too much to bear. Jean immediately ran to my right side, and Brenda immediately ran to my left, just as they have always done to hold me up; better yet, to carry me. My sister and I spent precious time, kissed, and reassured my sweet son before he took a flight to be with the angels. We laid my son to rest with love and affection together. We are on this journey together, holding each other up during the worst of times. We have all been wounded deeply by all the loss that we as a family have experienced. Somehow, they have always found a way to be my Wounded Healers.

Tiffany Jordan

Tiffany attended Lane College and Cleveland State University. It was at Morgan State University that she received her Master's in Compliance Administration Certification. Personally, and professionally, she has supported minority, women, and locally owned businesses for over twenty years. Her true passion is working with young adults, giving career and life advice.

AUGUST 7TH

Tiffany Jordan

I have always had an interesting, fun, make lemonade type of life. As a young girl around the age of 8, I discovered I had two basic life principles: (1) I will have good days and bad, and (2) There is a God, and he would always work for my good. In 1989, I unexpectedly became a teen Mom. I could not have been more disappointed in myself. Once again, I remembered my two basic life principles and employed them. I gave birth to a beautiful baby girl, Jasmine Victoria Jordan, born on January 27. I did not realize Jasmine was an angel that was on loan to me and was sent to save my life. However, I knew I had to take good care of God's gift. Her education was my top priority. I read to Jasmine daily, and if I did not, she would make sure I did by bringing me a book and saying, "read me a story." Jasmine went on to excel in school, graduating Valedictorian and later receiving dual degrees from Case Western Reserve University. Jasmine returned to Case employed as Dean of Undergraduate Admissions.

Jasmine was an avid traveler. She took her first plane ride at the age of five. She continued to travel the United States, the Islands, and throughout Europe. With the coaching of Constance Haqq, Jasmine decided to pursue her dream of living in Europe. Jasmine was bilingual and lived in Madrid, Spain, teaching elementary school children English as a second language for a few years. Jasmine returned to the States and was employed at Wright Patterson Air Force Base in Dayton, Ohio.

August 7, 2017, was a typical day at work for me. I went to lunch with my co-worker and had a brief conversation with Jasmine at that time. I left work at 3:30. I called Jasmine several times. Then at 3:35, I received a call that changed my life forever! The voice on the other end of the telephone asked where I was and what I was doing? I could tell it was not a good call. I was then informed Jasmine passed away from an "alleged suicide" at the age of 28.

Devastated with disbelief and rocked to my core, I had lost my only daughter and best friend. Jasmine was popular, respectful, and kind. Due to her popularity, and to my dismay, the news of her passing went out over social media. Another low blow was I had no privacy, and some people were unimaginably disrespectful. We decided to hold a private service for close friends and family. During Jasmine's service, I spoke about several things as it related to Jasmine's life. I shared that I was not exempt from the pain of losing a child, as many parents, unfortunately, came before me. I also shared this is - why we pray. Going to church is like going to baseball practice. How are you going to prove who you are in your darkest hour? How are you going to prove to God that you believe in him and that you were paying attention to his teaching?

My Mother has always been the rock for Jasmine and I. Mom was in the 4th stage of breast cancer, only later to pass away from a broken heart. My entire family was grieving; I only had myself to talk to, which was not good.

What I did not realize there was another angel by my side the entire time. Constance Haqq was not only someone I worked with; she gave me a great deal of professional and personal guidance because God knows I needed it. Constance is a woman who has always opened her heart and home to many women. Jasmine and I just happened to be a few of the lucky ones to spend time in Constance's light. I came to work daily because I needed to have a sense of normalcy. Honestly, I am not sure what I would have done alone. Constance was on the phone and in my office several times a day. She allowed me to voice my darkest secrets and simply cry. Constance provided me with trust and a safe place to talk. She connected me with a therapist and introduced me to another Mother who lost a child. I could never repay her for the time and resources she shared with me. Constance has what I call "the perfect temperature," never overbearing and always available. Constance nourished my mind, body, and spirit. From the day I met Constance, I admired everything about her, from her love of fashion to her love of people. Yes, there have been times when Constance would strongly recommend that I do something personally or professionally that I did not agree with. However, I would complete the task, and the outcome would be favorable, to which she would respond, "I told you so."

Monique Williams-Kelly

Monique Williams Kelly, MSSA, is a Growth and Impact Strategist, Motivational Speaker, Adjunct Instructor, CEO of the Engagement Group, Founder of Monique, Inc., Curator of Make It Happen Mondays, and a proud mother! Monique has learned how to truly achieve success - which is all about claiming power and walking in purpose. Monique earned a Bachelor of Arts in Journalism and Mass Communications from Kent State University, a Master of Science in Social Administration, and a Nonprofit Management Certification from Case Western Reserve University. She began her career in the non-profit sector, serving as an advocate for her community. Monique has recently launched Monique Inc., a consulting and coaching agency. It helps mid to senior-level female leaders of color in non-profits, social enterprises, or ministry let go of limiting beliefs, reignite their passion and purpose, and empower themselves to be impactful change-makers.

For more information about Monique, visit moniquewilliamsinc.com

NO CRYSTAL STAIR

Monique Williams-Kelly

"Life for me ain't been no crystal stair." That's what Langston Hughes said, and man, do I feel like he was writing about me! You see, I had managed to escape sexual abuse, neglect, rape, gang affiliation, and everything within my upbringing and environment that tried to break me. I graduated high school on time and went off to college – the first one in my family to pursue higher education. It was likely a bit of a surprise to my family and all the teachers I had given hell to over my high school years.

Nevertheless, there I was, a junior at Kent State University, active on campus, on the Dean's List, and a newly-inducted member of Delta Sigma Theta Sorority Inc. Seven other women and I made it! I could not stand them at first. My life up to that point had taught me to trust no one, and love came at a cost. I didn't want to be close to them, or anyone for that matter. I arrived on that campus angry, bitter, and unaware of the deep pain I carried with me, even though I thought I had escaped home. But now, I'm a sorority girl, a junior in college, and ready to take on the world. About a month after joining Delta, I realized my monthly cycle was late. There I was, 20 years old and pregnant, thinking, "Not me!" But then again, why not because life for me ain't been no crystal stair. I cried, played Lauren Hill's song, To Zion, and made a decision to keep my child. I gave up the Delta president seat I was to hold, and throughout my pregnancy, I went to a class in the morning and worked the third shift. I went in and out of the hospital with pre-term contractions until my first love was born five weeks early. I was a college student, single mother, and my entire family was two hours away. My commitment to him was to raise him as if I did it "right." Every night, at the same time, I bathed, rocked, and read to my son. I slowly but surely learned how to become a mother and learned how to love. We moved into an apartment that I paid for with my tuition refund check. I signed up for all the assistance programs I could and buckled down to finish courses I hadn't been able to complete over the year. When my son was about six months old, I had to take him to daycare. I couldn't keep taking him to my classes because I had nowhere else for him to go. I packed a huge bin with everything he could have needed and dropped him off. When I left, I stood outside the door and cried hysterically, but I pushed through it. I went back later that day to pick him up, and he was lying in the crib. He turned to me with the saddest look in his eyes, a huge teardrop, and a quivering lip. In that moment, he said in his face what he didn't have the ability to say with his words. I picked him up and told the daycare staff he would not be coming back. I had no idea what I would do, but after sharing what happened with my sorority sister, she said, "I'll change my classes tonight so you can go to your classes during the day, and I will keep him." This single act of sacrifice and kindness is why I graduated from college on time with my Bachelor's degree and my 15-month-old son on my hip. My baby thrived with her. He was loved and cared for, which gave me the peace of mind I needed to finish my degree and lay the foundation for our future. He became my motivation - my why. Since the time I learned of my pregnancy, I had seven women in my corner that supported me every day – through encouragement, dropping off ginger ale and saltine crackers, and pushing me to show up as a leader on campus even though I was with child. What I didn't realize at the time is that God gave me sisters right there in Kent that became my family. They were my backbone, inspiration, and my lifeline. Eighteen years later, it is still this way.

Sisters make the good times better
and the hard times easier.
(author unknown)

S. Cornelia Smith Kendrick

S. Cornelia Smith Kendrick holds a Master of Science degree in Social Administration (MSSA) and a Bachelor of Arts from Case Western Reserve University Mandel School of Applied Social Science and the College of Arts and Sciences respectively. She served for ten years in the United States Marine; which taught her the value of honor, standards, discipline, teamwork, and tenacity. As a veteran case manager with ten years of field experience, she has a common foothold to serve any population. Her academic achievements have been tempered with community volunteer service to veterans, returning citizens, and the Boy Scouts.

ENTER THE BEAUMONSTERS

S. Cornelia Smith Kendrick

I am a strong woman. Not only am I the mother of two, grandmother of two, daughter, sister, and veteran of the United States Marine Corps, but I am both a college and post-college graduate of Case Western Reserve University. I have experienced many accomplishments, failures, highs, lows, and in between. My children and grandchildren are most treasured by me; family is everything. What brings me to this writing is my membership in a club that no parent ever wants to become a member of - someone who has lost a child. I remember that terrible day as though it were yesterday. It is forever etched in my memory. My daughter was taken from me. She was snatched from her two beautiful children's lives when they were only 3 and 5 years old. My girl was a beautiful soul that loved her children with her entire heart. She was smart, beautiful, caring, and an amazing human being! July 28, 2015, was the day I died a little. I also fell apart a lot!

Someone murdered her that she once loved and that claimed to love her. A man that had been her fiancée, but the engagement had been broken. It was broken because he was broken, and he was broken by his experiences in the Air Force. He suffered from Post-Traumatic Stress Disorder (PTSD), something that too many of our men and women who serve our country face alone. In his twisted mind taking her life and his own was far better than confronting life without her.

Grieving is a difficult process, especially when you cannot wrap your mind around a situation. It felt like an out-of-body experience for me. I could not sleep or eat, yet I was expected to make decisions when no one should be making decisions. There was so much to do for the last time we would ever see her. Would we have a traditional service? Do we cremate? Where do we hold services? Which casket, style, and color? I was forced to make these mind-numbing decisions in the midst of grieving. There were no instructions because she was only 34, she had her entire life ahead of her, or so she thought. I was at my wit's end. I was crying, praying, seeking God's face, and pleading for direction. I was so very hurt for the children losing an amazing mother, losing my baby, and this senseless loss of life. I leaned on my faith in God, and He brought me through. I prayed that help would come. Then, my earthbound angels flew in! The Beaumonsters swooped in and made me feel loved and supported. They gave so freely, and I was so broken; all I could do was receive. I was a mess, and they held me up on all sides. They walked me through the moment and made sure their sister looked amazing, and her service was breathtaking. These were my daughter's friends from high school. Beaumonster is a term of endearment for the attendees and graduates of Beaumont High School. They are more than alumni; they are a family of women that love and support one another. These amazing women did not miss a beat or wait to be asked. They took the lead and did not allow their fallen sister to be neglected or her mother left to get things together on her own. These incredible women stood in the gap during the most difficult time of my life. We cried together and shared memories of her. These wonderful women kept a smile on my face. Let me be clear about the awesome task they took upon themselves; they prepared the service in its entirety. They ordered the flowers, made the programs, created a pictorial slideshow to music, provided music during the homegoing service, and so, so much more. I am still in awe of their professionalism and proficiency during that time. They called me to make sure I was ok, and to this day, they still check in on me. I lost my daughter that I birthed into this world, and I will forever grieve her absence. But I have gained daughters that help to fill the void of her passing. I now have amazing, professional, successful women who choose to call me "mom." For a few, I am privileged to fill the void that their mothers left when they made the transition to paradise. They will not allow my child, their friend, and fellow classmate to be forgotten and continue to ensure her memory is kept alive. I will forever be grateful and in their debt, because they rescued me from drowning. To be a Beaumonster is forever because it extends beyond this life!

Message to the reader: Live your life by these rules, put God first, and He will supply all your needs according to His riches in glory. Never settle for being pedestrian or ordinary, be extraordinary! Be the lion that ate the wolf. Do not talk about it, be about it! Take life by the horns and shake it till you get from it what you need. Compete with only you. Be the best version of yourself. Never apologize for having boundaries and enforcing them. Live life like there is no tomorrow because it is not. Love is a verb! Lastly, love the people God gave you because He will want them back one day.

Durecia Moorer

Durecia Moorer is a passionate entrepreneur with visionary leadership. As a Managing Partner and Chief Marketing Officer at ABCD & Company, Moorer leads marketing, media relations, and strategic partnerships. Her ability to drive stakeholder engagement has positioned ABCD as a recognized brand in the D.C. metro region. She is a recognized civic leader with a passion for youth engagement. At Heritage Fellowship Church, Moorer serves as the Minister of Youth and a member of the Stewardship Committee—serving on the Education Subcommittee. She is the Co-founder of Diamonds in the Rough, Inc., a Cleveland nonprofit organization dedicated to supporting young urban girls.

She is a proud Howard University alumna, holds a Master of Science in Management, and is pursuing a second Masters from the Samuel DeWitt Proctor School of Theology at Virginia Union University. In her free time, she enjoys baking, mentoring, and spending time with family and friends. Durecia is a native of Cleveland, Ohio, and resides in Northern Virginia.

A BRIDGE OVER TROUBLED WATER

Durecia Moorer

There are times when God brings blessings the way that you can't see, nor do you feel that you are worthy of them. I am a woman who has experienced imposter syndrome and, in some instances, outright refused to walk in those blessings because of how they came. In some seasons, regardless of my accolades, work ethic, or gifting, there were times when I felt that I could never measure up to God's promises. I thought those blessings should be contingent on what I did and not simply His mercy and grace. It is why the only way I felt accomplished was if I perfectly executed something. It was clearly demonstrated that I was a worthy candidate for the blessings and ultimately to be used by God.

In my sophomore year in college, I strived for that perfection and to attain a closer walk with God. I studied the Bible diligently and tried my best to fit into the perfect box of what it means to be a Christian. My efforts rewarded me, but there were times that I didn't feel I was my authentic self. Little did I know, there was someone who saw the blessing that I needed and was praying for me. While I am choosing to keep this person's name anonymous, I can't deny the indelible impact she has had on my life and how she has been a bridge for me over troubled waters.

Those troubled waters, for me, manifest themselves in the form of internal conflict. At the time, I attempted to understand what God was doing in my life. God not only disrupted my plans, but He altered what I thought was my purpose and destiny. He totally uprooted everything I thought I ever knew about Him and where I was headed in life. In that season, I felt isolated and alone. I couldn't conceptualize why as a college student, I was experiencing such uncomfortable and trying circumstances. One day I reached out to this woman. The same woman who met me where I was in high school and allowed me to find my way was present once again. She helped to lay such an incredible foundation for my life as a Christian. Here I was, reaching out for a lifeline and hoping that whatever she shared would be the clarity that I needed to move forward. Yet, I was reminded of God's promises for my life.

That call forever changed my life. She didn't have to send me a care package, put money on my tuition, or purchase a few books. The words of wisdom that she shared put me in alignment with my purpose and prepared me for what was to come. I think what was so significant about that moment was; she made time for me; she always made time for me. Although most of those instances were through a quick phone conversation after I left home from college, she has always been there—as a spiritual compass and a guiding light to bring clarity to my life and purpose. It is for that reason that I am grateful. I know I would not be the God-fearing woman I am today if it wasn't for her nurturing and compassionate spirit to always be willing and available.

I am the Lord who heals you – Exodus 12:26

A sister can be seen as someone who is both ourselves and very much not ourselves. A special kind of double.

-Toni Morrison

Ebony Brown-Muhammad

Ebony Brown-Muhammad is a 48-year-old native of Akron, Ohio. She is a mother of 7, a homemaker, and a homeschooler. Ebony's lifetime passion has been to help others feel good and be happy. With her love of baking, she has made a name for herself with her baked goods and catering business, Mother's Food Service. Famous for her well-known chicken pasta salad, she enjoys offering healthy choices for her customers. Ebony is a Certified Herbal Specialist and is studying for her Master's degree in Herbal Science. She is also a Dried Blood Cell Analyzer and practitioner. She is a Certified Gold Seal Scientology Dianetics Auditor and Superior. She works for Akron Public Schools in the Child Nutrition Services Department. Ebony is a 2nd level Chi Gong student practicing energy healing. She enjoys using her gift of singing to heal and help others with difficulty coping with life challenges. She has been in the Ministry class of the Nation of Islam and instructor for the Muslims Girls in Training class for eight years.

BREAKING THE CHAINS OF MENTAL BONDAGE

Ebony Brown-Muhammad

"I am free!" I screamed these words as I drove down the expressway, away from the cave of darkness. I was no longer afraid to be alone or to be a single mom. I wasn't scared anymore to hit rock bottom with no money, no home, and a broken-down vehicle. I was on the road to peace of mind and safety. I never imagined my life spiraling down the "generational curse" road of being a single black female with many children and insecure about my future. I never thought of myself being dependent on government programs to SURVIVE. No. I gave my word to myself, even if only in a whisper, and dared not to speak it aloud for my mom and aunties to hear. That would be judgmental of them absent compassion or understanding of circumstances, which led me right to the lifestyle I spoke so harshly about as a teenager. I realized at that moment that I was walking in Hagar's shoes.

For the past 20 years, I ran back and forth with the thought my marriage was over. I did not want to admit or accept it. I compromised my singing gift, my love for baking, and public speaking, for my marriage. Everything I did became subject to my husband's approval and validation. I believed if I did not get his attention, it was worthless. I had become and embraced being a victim.

In my mother's one-bedroom apartment, the first night of freedom, I cried silently while watching over my daughters. We were free from the bondage of being suffocated by the subliminal cloud that said we were not good enough. I fought through a deep depression for a month - not eating, long nights of mental anguish, and aberrated self-talk. I did not know who was talking in my head. Were these his thoughts and ideas? Yes, they were. I had to reach out for help. I could not hide behind the image of the good sister soldier who had it all together. I was a partner in a thirty-year marriage, faithful believer, charitable and dependable Muslim, and part of the dreadful under the link 'Muslims don't divorce.' Nadiyah was there to help me stand up again. She was there to hear my tears without any conversation. I was able to get the hurt out and still look at myself as a child of Allah (God). I did not care how I looked on the outside because the pain on the inside was an inner aching that I never felt before. It could not be compared to the pain of childbirth, a broken bone, or a breakup. Heartbreak is traumatic. It oozes on and is consistent, regardless of the time of day or the obstacles I was facing. It was painful to walk, sit, take a shower or open my mouth to speak. The verbal convictions from my ex-husband kept playing over and over in my head. I was in and out of present time consciousness and knew I had to do something. I reached out to a woman whom I was divinely drawn to visit just from a Facebook communication in 2016. As a result of our communications, I flew to Florida by invitation to a life-changing event. Nayyirah is an angel from heaven. I was not acquainted with her personality or family history as I would most of my friends. It's that very clear intuitive connection that lets me know I can trust her with my life. She was always asking me to wake up and be alive. Or she would ask, "Did you hear me? Let me say it again." Nayyirah would call me at my lowest points, check on me and invite me to study something or travel with her. I did not have the nerve to tell her what was going on, but my intuition told me she already knew. God works through men and especially women.

Out of touch with Facebook for about a year, I logged on to find she was offering life coaching appointments. I booked immediately. Our session was so spiritually attuned and accurate. I opened by stating my present situation, and she took the wheel. It was like God removed her voice and her mind and spoke directly to me. I instantly felt a release from that moment. I had clarity and confidence restored that I thought I would never have again. I believed in ME and now possessed the willingness to nurture my own healing. I am grateful for the struggle and the victory over the loss of my marriage of thirty years. I can testify to the power of prayer, patience, and Allah's (God's) tender love after coming through it. He was always there; I only had to keep walking towards Him with complete childlike trust in HIM. I have learned valuable lessons transforming me into a better daughter, mother of 7, sister, and Muslim.

Sadie Muhammad

Sadie Muhammad is a native of Youngstown, Ohio. She is married to Louis Muhammad and a proud mother of six children. She is Founder, and Chief Executive Officer of "Somebody's Gotta Do It Cleaning Services." She also owns Hair Wiggle, a local beauty salon in Youngstown. She serves as Co-Chair for "Helping Healing Hands," a nonprofit organization that helps mothers of murdered children help others by sharing their stories. She created the "MEWE" clothing line, whose profits benefit women impacted by domestic violence. Mrs. Muhammad holds a Bachelor of Arts degree in Pre-Law and Political Science, with a minor in Criminal Justice from Youngstown State University. She is also a Phi Beta Gamma member, an organization for individuals working in the legal field.

FIGHTING BUT NOT LOSING

Sadie Muhammad

The wounds are hidden deep, but the story behind them all will forever be a blessing. The molestation, the abusive relationships, and suicide attempt are just what someone might need to hear. The month of October in 1996 will forever be the deepest wound anyone could ever experience. It was then that my mother was found shot to death in her home, lying face down in a pool of blood. With bullet holes in her back, her hands were shot off from trying to protect her face. The moment I arrived at the scene, her body had already been removed. I clearly remember the hour. I was in complete shock. I stood outside and looked up at the sky and slowly closed my eyes, asking God, "WHY?"

As a little girl, I remember my mom allowing cousins to live with us because their mom had thrown them out. My mom owned a bar and often came home very late. It was during this time that my male cousin would enter my room and begin tugging at my underwear. Once I was awake, he would place his hand over my mouth. I was so afraid of telling my mom because I knew she would literally kill him - my mom was a known gun carrier and a street fighter who went to battle for her children. My parents later divorced, I went to live with my dad and his wife. This woman was nothing but pure evil. She would pretend to be caring and loving, but at every turn, she would beat and slap a ten-year-old little girl for no apparent reason. She would grab iron skillets and hit me in the head and back; thank God I was a sprinter. This woman hit me in my eye while asleep. I jumped to my feet but could not open my eye. The harder I tried, it just kept watering with an intense burning that wouldn't stop. She took me to the hospital and told the doctor I was playing basketball, and the ball hit me in the face. This abuse lasted for years. My father and I do not communicate because of his blatant decision to ignore how this woman chose to treat me.

My relationship with the male gender was just hideous due to the fact that as a little girl, I never witnessed healthy interactions from my parents toward each other and not enough with me. I experienced low self-esteem that brought on the depression, which caused me to look for love in all the wrong places. These so-called love relationships birthed children who were now part of a reality that was completely unstable. I kept going in and out of drama and self-pity; the list is endless. One day I found myself on the top of a five-level parking deck, getting ready to jump off. I would have never survived that fall. I was admitted to the hospital for a while. I had to once again face demons, anger, and pain from all tunnels of my mind. I can tell my story today and never be ashamed. As Marvin Sapp expresses, "Never would have made it . . .". I have countless individuals to give thanks and praise to for helping me, but one person, in particular, was extremely helpful. I will call her Sister Muhammad (I don't know her first name), and she was a member of The Nation of Islam. I never told her, but her humble spirit and skill that encouraged me just simply to tell my story and how it all happened was a breath of fresh air and made all the difference at the beginning of my healing. Her gentle spirit of wanting to get me through the session called "auditing," hosted by The Church of Scientology, in Chicago, Illinois, on behalf of The Honorable Minister Louis Farrakhan, is all that I needed as she carried me from my beginning all the way up to the point of our session. She was so persistent and careful in her treatment of me.

Despite my trauma and wounds, only almighty God allowed me to stay grounded. There is so much more work to do on me, but I have made many strides. I created a brand of clothing titled

"MEWE" - What happens to "me" affects the "we." This brand supports women impacted by domestic violence and abuse. It also offers, more importantly, education on self-love and cares for themselves. I have had the blessing along with the pleasure of hosting gatherings where women have shared their pain, tears, and joys of overcoming. I have learned to focus on the process and the power of forgiveness, not the pain. I have also learned that it is not what happens to you in life; it's how you interpret what happens.

"Rise above emotions into the thinking of God."
The Honorable Minister Louis Farrakhan

Lori Williams-Murphy

Lori started her education at the Cleveland Metropolitan School District. She worked for nine years as a family liaison, T.E.A.M.S. (Teaching and Educating Against the Misuse of Drugs) coordinator, and Girl Power! Advisor. In January of 2012, Lori accepted the Concierge position at Cuyahoga Community College's District Administration Building. She began to volunteer and became the Mentoring Co-chair for the Black American Council department; she also served as a mentor to more than ten students.

Lori's passion for youth inspired her to create the Annual Tri-C, Stuff the Bus with Fox 8 News initiative. Tri-C has stuffed the bus with over 575 boxes of school supplies and donated more than 3,500 personalized Tri-C book bags to the Kids-In-Need resource center in Cleveland, Ohio. During her five years at the District Administrative Office, Lori received her Associate of Applied Science degree with a concentration in Human Service and her Associate of Arts degree. She maintained a 3.5 grade point average and graduated cum laude.

To contact Lori, email, msann1026@gmail.com

IF YOU JUST BELIEVE

Lori Williams-Murphy

On September 11, 2001, I drove down Superior Avenue to John D. Rockefeller K-8 School for a job interview with Edna D. Connally, the Principal. During my nervous travel, I looked around to see if any tall buildings in Cleveland, Ohio, had been hit by terrorist-operated airplanes, like the Twin Towers in New York. My anxiety level was elevated. I was sure my blood pressure had reached the 150/90 mark because my heart was racing, and my depression had an enormous grip on my thoughts. I prayed, "God, please help me with my life and this interview. In Jesus name, Amen." Upon arriving at the building, I developed enough enthusiasm to enter the door with a smile on my face. I walked into the office, where I met Mrs. Connally. I had heard that she was a tough, no-nonsense leader; I was already feeling discouraged, so again, I asked God to step in and take over. If I had put my self-esteem on a scale of 1-10, it would have been a zero. To be honest, I was only attending this interview because my sister, Jacqueline Williams-Payne, and my best friend, Kelly Greene-Eads, believed in me. They had more faith in me than I had in myself. My depression, sadness, and fear kept me stagnant most of the time, and it was hard for me to see the blessings that had been bestowed upon my life. All I wanted to do was feel normal, whatever that felt like.

She invited me into her office, and we began to talk. Every question she asked, I answered to the best of my ability and honestly. I believed my high school diploma would not allow me to maintain a job in a school district, not to mention having no experience with computers. "God, why am I here?" I am sure this Principal is going to wave me out of her office as soon as I start talking about my experience - but she did not. After interviewing me for thirty minutes, she asked me, did I really want the position, and I said, "Yes." She looked at me and stated, "I will contact H.R. tomorrow." I stood up with a smile, thanked her, shook her hand, and walked out of her office.

That day I learned that my thoughts were suffocating me. On October 1, 2001, I started my new job. I continued to struggle with my fears, which I saw as failures. In my mind, every adult person working at John D. Rockefeller K-8 School was well-educated except for me. I was ashamed and embarrassed by what I had not done with my life. I wanted to avoid certain activities because I did not want anyone to know my secrets, at least the ones that kept me in the judgment of myself. As time went on, Mrs. Connally put me in charge of events that I wanted no parts. I had to attend all in-house engagements and external community events. That same year I created a parent committee that later received a $5,000.00 award from the C.E.O. of the school district to gift students who passed all five parts of their proficiency test. Twenty-five students were awarded Play Stations or bicycles. In February 2004, I coordinated my first Black History program, where more than six hundred students, staff, and parents were in attendance. Yet, I still struggled with my capabilities. I worked for Mrs. Connally for the next four years, and under her leadership and tutelage, I grew. She helped me to overcome some fears and insisted I confront assignments that I dreaded. She coached me to the level that enabled me to believe I mattered. In her presence, she would not allow me to look back at what I had not accomplished.

In 2010, I was laid off from the Cleveland Metropolitan School District. Edna continued to work for the district and retired a few years later after 35 years of service. She then became Rev. Dr. Edna D. Connally; her continued support over the years has helped me to believe that whatever I put my mind to, I could achieve it. I just had to believe in M.E.! I learned to trust God because He makes no mistakes. Besides, I was created in His image, so I am unique! Today, I love myself; I matter. I am not perfect by any means, and I do not have everything that I want in life. But I do have my self-esteem, faith, and the courage to continue the mission that God put me on to help others. Today, I work at Cuyahoga Community College, where their mantra is, "Where Futures Begin." I am now God's wounded healer! Rev. Dr. Edna D. Connally was the vessel that God used to help me strive for academic growth and self-esteem, which helped me believe the apostle Paul's words, "I can do all things through Christ who strengthens me." (Philippians 4:13, K.J.V.).

If you are always trying to be normal you will never know how amazing you can be.
– Dr. Maya Angelo

Patricia Price

Patricia Price enjoys caring for and helping others. She is blessed to work in an industry that speaks to her passion and is extremely rewarding. For the past sixteen years, she has worked as a Residential Coordinator to care for individuals with intellectual disabilities. She is forty-four years old, an only child, and was born and raised in the city of Cleveland, Ohio. She enjoys spending time with her husband and family members.

FAVOR & MERCY

Patricia Price

I was an only child with both my Mom and Dad in the home. My parents worked and provided a loving family for me. Life was good until the age of six years old. That's when I spent the night at a friend's home. During the night, I was awakened by her older brother, who was nine years older than me, with his hand over my mouth and laying on top of me, telling me not to say anything to anyone. I finally cried myself to sleep and did exactly what he told me - I didn't tell anyone. A few years passed, and I returned to the friend's house again to play. We would play "house." Her older sister, who was the twin of the brother who previously violated me, would play with us. She would say, "Trisha, you are my husband." I did not think much of it since we were playing. She made me do unspeakable things. This went on for a few years. As time went on, I became used to these unfortunate acts; so much so that it began to seem normal. Again, I told no one.

I excelled in my schoolwork in elementary school, earning my spot on the honor roll, and rarely missed school unless I was ill. When I was roughly ten, my parents began having issues and decided to divorce. My Dad moved out, and I stayed with my Mom. I noticed things starting to change. My Mom wasn't going to work anymore, our telephone was disconnected, and a few weeks later, my Mom started getting rid of our furniture. Shortly after that, we no longer had a home. We moved into a one-bedroom house with my 20-year-old aunt, her husband, and son. This was my first experience of losing my Mom. My Mom would leave me with my aunt so that she could be with her new boyfriend. At times I wouldn't see her for a couple of days. I wasn't being taken to school on a regular basis anymore. Many nights I was not able to sleep due to the adults partying. I was not accustomed to this. I went to visit my Dad one weekend and decided I would not return to my Mom. I wanted to be somewhere that reminded me of how things used to be; somewhere peaceful, a bed of my own, and away I'd be able to get to and from school.

As the years went by, I was again faced with being violated. This time it was a family member, a cousin. I could not understand why these things were happening to me. This time I told someone. However, nothing happened. No one believed me. The violations continued for a few years. When my Mom and her boyfriend got their place, I would visit on weekends and spend summers with her. My parents' parenting styles were different. My Dad was strict, but my Mom was not. At the age of fifteen, I went to visit my Mom for the summer. I got pregnant. I only told my friends. It was almost five months when my Dad found out. It was an extremely difficult and confusing time. One minute I was told I could keep the baby; the next minute, I could not. I really didn't want to get rid of my baby, but I had an abortion. Due to how far along I was, I had a procedure that was basically giving birth to a still-born child. I had to stay overnight in the hospital. I felt so alone and helpless. Yes, my Dad was there, and my Grandmother called to check in on me. However, I wanted my Mom, and she didn't even call. My Mom and I continued to have a rocky relationship. We would disagree and argue a lot as I still felt she was putting her boyfriend's needs before mine. I dropped out of school at the age of eighteen.

During the following year, my Mom and I seemed to be growing closer, and I began to understand things better. But on July 20, 1996, my life would forever change. I had spoken to my Mom several times that morning. Each time we both shared how much we loved each other. Later that evening, my uncle called and told me my Mom had been killed in a car accident. From that moment on, I would never be the same. I became so angry and bitter. I couldn't understand why my Mom was taken from me again. I spiraled out of control. For about eight years, I didn't seem to care about much of anything. I was partying, drinking, being very promiscuous, and had low self-esteem. Of course, there were times when I wanted to do something different; find a way to better myself. However, I could never stay committed to changing.

In June of 2004, I started a new job. What I didn't know was that I would meet a woman who would be such a wonderful mentor - Mrs. G. She was much more than my Director. She took time with me and truly got to know me. She encouraged me and helped me understand self-love. I got my high school diploma, and because of her encouraging me, I had the guts to apply for two different positions and received the promotions both times. She saw in me what I couldn't see in myself at the time. She always made herself available no matter the day or time. She taught me so much more than being a Residential Manager. She taught me to accept and love myself. Most of all, she showed me that I was worth more than what I had experienced. For all of my life's experiences, I will forever be grateful.

Ilinda Reese

International speaker and author Ilinda Reese specialize in lifting the weights loaded on women who want to unlearn, unlock and unleash their core so they can flourish, live abundantly and leave a legacy for their family. Reese demonstrates how a shift in perspective can shift your experiences. Reese inspires hope, healing, and moving you from gridlock to greatness.

FINDING LIGHT IN DARKNESS: AN INTIMATE INTERGRATIONAL JOURNEY TO HEALING

Ilinda Reese

When I thought of my contribution to "Wounded Healer," I was immediately confronted with the dilemma that specific other contributors faced. The very definition of dilemma, a situation in which a difficult choice has to be made between two or more alternatives of equals, explains the challenge. The request sent me to a place where I had to give careful thought to my life's women influencers. Though I cannot go deep into the process, my choice resonated with me as my space is limited. Though I have been known to be a Healer (someone who helps you find your own ability to heal), I had to study the times when I, as a Wounded Healer, needed someone to help me heal, so I crossed generations to settle on my selection. My choice is one who is unassuming and will wonder in her mind why she was selected.

She is humble and comfortable staying in the background until called upon. First and foremost, she loves God and studies the word for understanding and guidance. She is a seeker of knowledge, and unlike many young people, she is willing to listen and learn. Whether learning the word or researching healthy living, she goes all in, taking voracious notes and changing her lifestyle to embrace her new level of thinking. Her passion led to my selection of her becoming my accountability partner and adjusting and prioritizing my lifestyle. We created a slogan that says, "no sweets during the week," as a reminder for me when faced with the temptation of eating sweets. As a result, I only eat sweets on the weekend, and the mental discipline worked.

My influential woman is teachable, and to be teachable is an admirable quality that will take her to her destiny.

My Healer, though she has no children of her own, surrounds herself with youth and pours her life into them, taking them places, connecting with them, and providing experiences from which they can learn—having a keen sense of humor always helps when spending time with children and the youth. She laughs freely, heartedly, easily, and enjoys a joyful space. Her spirit is sensitive, compassionate, and observant. When you are the focus of her attention, you feel like you matter.

On the day my father, Pastor L.W. Boone, went home to be with the Lord, I remember being overcome with grief. There were few words and little comfort that would suffice. Thinking back, I will never forget, my Healer crawled up in bed with me, wrapped her arms around, and held me while I cried until we both fell asleep. She spoke no words and understood that none were needed. Having lost her father, who was her best friend, as a young adult, and my younger brother, she knew how it felt to need someone to lean on while hurting. While not having physical access to her father, she has had many struggles that would teach her resilience and give her the ability to bounce back. If you were to ask her how she feels about me, she would tell you, perhaps, how I pour into her life being her elder; however, she would be unaware of how much she gives to me. And though I tell her how she lifts my spirit during our frequent conversations, she has yet to see and understand her worth. She is a healer that has the ability to heal the wounded healer, and I am forever grateful. Every opportunity I am given to look internally to heal increases my capacity to heal others. Thank you...' Shawntee.'

Charmaine Rice

Charmaine Rice is a proud contributor to the Wounded Healer compilation of stories of resilience and community. She has two sons; Kieran, a computer engineer who resides in Austin, Texas, and Keon, a high school senior who balances a rigorous course load with a part-time job and basketball. She is celebrating her second chance at love in the form of a recent marriage to her husband and best friend, Kelly Rice Sr., and her newly expanded family network. A lifelong learner, Charmaine is a graduate of the Cleveland Bridge Builders class of 2020. She previously earned a Master's degree from Cleveland State University in Psychology with a specialization in Diversity Management and Organizational Leadership. Charmaine earned a Bachelor's degree from Wright State University in Communications with a specialization in Public Relations. She is a member of the Board of Trustees for the Cleveland Leadership Center and a member of the Ohio Diversity Council's Cleveland Advisory Board. An administrator, facilitator, and coach for many programs and topics, Charmaine has proven that an intentional focus on diversity and inclusion can inspire innovation and is the secret to sustainable success for individuals, communities, teams, and organizations.

LESSONS FROM DEBORAH

Charmaine Rice

"I believe you. The things that happened to you are not your fault. You will be ok; you are a survivor." If given a chance, these are the words I would say to my younger self. Darkness to Light, an organization committed to the research, education, and prevention of child sexual abuse, suggests that as many as "one in every ten children will experience sexual abuse before their 18th birthday." This translates to an estimated 42 million adult survivors of child sexual abuse in the United States at the time of this writing. I am one of those survivors. The words that I began with are the messages that came to mind when I was encouraged by an aunt to consider what I would say to my younger self if given a chance. But what exactly is child sexual abuse? Most people know that child sexual abuse includes any sexual act between an adult and a minor – it includes forcing, coercing, or persuading a child to engage in any activity of a sexual nature. Many people don't know that child sexual abuse can also include non-contact activity such as exposure to sexually-themed images and communication. Although I was aware that his sinful acts were not my fault, my abuser would use verbal abuse to shift blame, threaten, or downplay his behavior by explaining how he was not crossing the ultimate line. As a young teenager, the abuse I endured taught me not to trust anyone and how to wear a mask to hide my emotional scars. As a coping strategy, I would regularly tell myself, "It could be worse." I began counting the days until I would be "free" or old enough to leave home. Every day I hoped and prayed for a way out. When I graduated high school, I left home. In moving away from my abuser at the first possible opportunity, I believed I would also leave behind the pain, feelings of shame, worthlessness, dirtiness, and overall lack of value. I was wrong.

I packed my bags and carried the pain, confusion, and scars with me into the next stage of my life. Unbeknownst to me, those bags included an inability to fully trust others. At the age of 19, I became a mother - a young mother who didn't have a relationship with my own mother. I was at a loss for a guide in this critical stage of life. Three months after my son's birth, one of my paternal aunts, concerned that I would spend the Easter holiday alone, connected me with family members who lived nearby - my maternal uncle Marcus and his wife, Debbie. Aunt Debbie was ten years older than me when we first connected. At 29, she was a young wife, mom of three, and former military. At that time, our age difference seemed significant. Because of how she handled the challenges in life and embraced the good, I thought she was so much older than me. I didn't have a car, so my aunt or uncle would often pick up my son and me, take us to spend time at their home, and then take us back home. Aunt Debbie never pressed me for information about my childhood experiences, but instead, she showed me the value of presence and family. Through her actions, she demonstrated what my son and I had not previously experienced. The way Aunt Debbie cared for her family and the manner in which she embraced me and my son - her husband's niece and great-nephew - provided me with an example of a woman being a respectful and respected advocate for her family. From the very first time I visited their home, Aunt Debbie carefully, patiently, and respectfully met me where I was and gently walked with me to a place of healing. She introduced me to scriptures about grace and forgiveness, messages that I needed for my own healing. Slowly, I began to open up and express vulnerability. With the assurance that I was in a safe space, I set my mask aside and began the work of healing from the inside out. Aunt

Debbie became my guide, my mentor, and my friend. She invited me to reflect on the messages I would give to my younger self. Our friendship restored elements of my faith that had tarnished. When I feel past doubts creep up, Aunt Debbie is my reminder that there is power in simply showing up, being consistent, and truly being present for other women. Aunt Debbie is a living example of the Ralph Waldo Emerson quote, "What you do speaks so loudly, that I cannot hear what you say."

A'bria Robinson

A'bria Robinson is the founder of BeYOUtiful Cleveland, which transforms young ladies, ages 10-18, through customized education plans, with an emphasis on fostering sisterhood. She hosts a free weekly sister circle program for young ladies to expose them to the knowledge of countless characteristics that improve young women's projectile. In 2016 A'bria Robinson was recognized by ICan Schools for her outstanding service to the Northeast Ohio communities. She also served as a consultant for United for Girls, an organization that fosters a commitment to young girls and promotes a positive self-image and a sense of hope through mentoring. A'bria is a recent graduate of John Carroll University, where she earned her bachelor's degree in Communication with a concentration in Marketing. A'bria is currently serving her community as a Family Life Specialist.

To contact A'bria, email, AbriaR@beyoutifulcle.org

GRANDMA'S HANDS

A'bria Robinson

It is with immense gratitude that I share the story of my beautiful Grandparents, Harvey and Elizabeth P. Green. It isn't easy to express the amount of love I felt from my Grandparents growing up, but I will say that their love inspired me to share this story with the world. For the sake of this story and Wounded Healer, my Grandmother is now yours. We call her "Ma-Ma." Starting with my Grandpa, as far back as I can remember, I was what anyone would call a "Grandpa's girl." I followed my Grandpa everywhere and practically worshipped the ground he walked on. He gave me unconditional love and taught me many lessons that still stick with me today. As I grew older, I realized that the lessons my Grandpa taught me started as a child. One of the earliest and silly lessons that he gave me was calling me "Big Girl." It was a silly but easy way to remind me to put my big girl pants on when facing a challenge. For example, when he taught me how to ride my first big girl bike, I remember going down the driveway fast with him right by my side. "Turn, big girl!" He said, and as I tried to turn, I lost control and fell. He came running to me and said, "It's okay, Big Girl, let's try it again." This same message echoed to me as he taught me how to drive. It's funny looking back because him calling me "Big Girl" actually made me feel like I could do anything! I could conquer whatever challenge that was coming my way. Another lesson I learned from him early on was selflessness. My Grandpa would literally give the clothes off his back to anyone who was in need. He was a very caring and loving person. Oftentimes people who knew him would say, "He never met a stranger." I can remember a time when Ma-Ma would say, "Harvey talks too much!" She'd say that because he literally knew everyone, and if he saw you, he'd make it his mission to let you know that he saw you. Although it was frustrating to Ma-Ma, it was one of the many reasons she and many others loved him.

As I reflect on my growth, I realize that the lessons he has instilled in me are molding me into a young woman who walks with the same courage, compassion, and love for people he, too, walked alongside. On March 6th of 2015, my senior year of high school, Grandpa passed away. On my way home from school, I received a call from my very distraught mother. I could hear the panic in her voice as she told me to "get home immediately." I rushed home anxious, nervous, and afraid. When I got home, I hurried into my Grandparents' room. I remember seeing my mother on our stairs and throwing my keys down, feeling something terrible had happened. Once I got into my Grandparents' room, I saw Ma-Ma pumping my Grandpa's chest, giving him CPR, all while holding the phone between her ear and shoulder speaking with the 911 operator. I froze at the door. No one had prepared me for what I was about to see. Grandpa was stretched out on the bed, lifeless. With every breath in her body, Ma-Ma gave her all to save my Grandpa's life. She pumped, prayed, and spoke with Grandpa as he transitioned into the next life. I was in shock. I know that we all will have our day to take our last breath eventually, but not my Grandpa. My Grandpa was to live forever, and certainly as long as I lived. While watching Ma-Ma pump his chest, I held his hand and talked to him. I didn't cry at the sight of his lifeless body; I was confused as to what was happening even though I knew. If that sentence lost you, that's exactly how I felt internally; I felt lost. Ma-Ma continued to pump his chest until the ambulance arrived. The paramedics came into the house and began to work on his body right in front of us. We all knew. Ma-Ma knew that Grandpa was gone, although they wouldn't pronounce it at home. She said, "I did all that I could." And she did. I was the only one in the room who saw her at that moment. I saw her focused, and I saw her dedicated to her husband's life. Ma-Ma didn't fall apart; she knew that she was needed and that God needed to use her.

The same hands that Ma-Ma pumped Grandpa's chest with, she used them to care for people as a nurse since 1958 in the city of Cleveland. Ma-Ma first began her work in nursing homes and eventually for private practice. I've been honored to watch her tend to and care for many people since my childhood. I've seen Ma-Ma in action, saving lives and caring for them before my Grandpa took his last breath. I always thought she had an intrinsic ability to know exactly what to do when it was needed. The truth is, Ma-Ma was trained. She was trained and guided by God her entire life. It amazes me how God has used her time and time again as a vessel to experience his love and care. Ma-Ma is the kind of woman who doesn't wish nor care for public acknowledgment. She is simply doing what she feels called to do. She's living the way that God wants her to live and without question. Ma-Ma served as a bridge to help me over the troubled waters of my Grandfather's passing. I was in a dark space after he passed. As a true lover of people, I can honestly say I did not want to see or talk to anyone. I was done. I was angry, frustrated, and with just about every negative emotion that you could imagine. Life had truly paused for me; I was stuck and had no idea how to get myself out of this dark hole. Although I still struggle with his physical absence, Ma-Ma taught me that life could not stop. She continues to teach me that although things happen, my purpose is still living and breathing in me. In the midst of her own grief and dealing with the death of her life partner and husband, Ma-Ma has cared for and carried me with her strength. She is an extraordinary painting of selflessness, and it makes sense why my Grandparents chose each other. I am so incredibly thankful for her life, love, and the many lessons that she continues to teach me. Ma-

Ma is the epitome of a virtuous woman. I wish that every human being would experience the love that I experienced from my Grandpa and the love that Ma-Ma continues to shower me with, as I feel so undeserving of the amount of love, she gives me. Now being older, I understand the reflection of God's love and grace. God loves me so much that he would bless me with the opportunity to experience such immense love from my Grandparents. The abundance of love and prayers that my beautiful Grandmother has over me led to the Women's Circle of Wisdom's birth. Through this monthly gathering, young women come to simply "be" and gain the wisdom of not only my Grandmother but the Mothers, Aunts, and Grandmothers all over the city of Cleveland. Women's Circle of Wisdom is a shared and intimate experience of sisterhood ACROSS GENERATIONS. My mission is to impact other young women and provide a safe space for healing, as Ma-Ma has done for me. With this story, Ma-Ma, I honor you and your life. Thank you to all of the Ma-Ma's of the world who carry and cover us in our time of need and heartache.

Message to the readers: May healing and love flow all through your body as you read these words and may your troubles cease at the end of where your journey of healing begins.

"Healing may not be so much about getting better, as about letting go of everything that isn't you – all of the expectations, all of the beliefs – and becoming who you are".

– Rachel Naomi Remen

Minister Sheila Smith

Sheila Smith is two-time breast cancer, bilateral mastectomy, lymphedema, and domestic violence survivor. Having been a victim of childhood molestation and rape, she now stands as a 51-year-old victorious Wounded Healer. She was born and raised in Flint, Michigan, and relocated to Atlanta, Georgia, at the age of 18 to attend college. She has an accounting and bookkeeping background. She has been happily married to Mario Smith for the last 18 years, and they have two beautiful daughters, Iyanna Smith, 16; and Arianna Smith, 13. Sheila has been a stay-at-home mom for the last 16 years, but her passion and heart for children have led her to serve as a professional volunteer within her local church and school district. Within this time, she has served on her local school council, PTA, and a dance team, track, and basketball mom. She loves serving God as an ordained minister at Redeeming Love Christian Church. Sheila is currently planning her non-profit organization's launch: Extended Arms - The Sheila L. Smith foundation.

To contact Sheila, email, sheilasmith1969@yahoo.com

A MOTHERS LOVE

Minister Sheila Smith

Every girl dreams of having her mother present in her life. She assumes that her mother will be present for her sweet 16 birthday celebration to help her pick out her prom dress, and of course, the ultimate beautiful cascading wedding gown. She assumes that her mother will be present for every milestone in her life. She believes that her mother will be there for her graduation, wedding, and most dear, her children's birth. Every girl thinks that her mother will be there to bail her out of trouble and hold her hand through her toughest and most challenging times. She welcomes her mother's comfort through her storms and expects her to be her light at the end of every dark tunnel.

A mother's wisdom, love, encouragement, and support are supposed to be a given. You just know she'll be there because she is always supposed to be. You are her heartbeat, the very core of her. These things that I just mentioned I never got to experience with my birth mother. As a teenager, I lost my mother to drugs, alcohol, and all the other things that come along with those forms of addiction. After all of that, there was cancer and then death. I always felt that life had not been kind to me. I felt I was dealt a horrible hand which left a hole in my heart. I was to face life alone, as a motherless child left to fend for herself.

In my mid 20's, I signed up to be a mentor of middle and high school-age girls through my church's mentoring program. I was extremely excited about contributing to the social & spiritual development of the young girls, especially since having had the bitter experience of navigating most of life's trials and tribulation without that kind of guidance of my mother.

During my time with the mentoring program, God was very

strategic in placing me directly under the director's leadership, Ms. Carolyn Jones Simmons. Ms. Carolyn Jones Simmons is a beautiful, God-fearing, breast, brain, and colon, cancer survivor. As a lead mentor, I had no idea that I would become her mentee and spiritual daughter. God was forming an everlasting relationship that His spirit and love would bond together.

As the years past Ms. Carolyn and I grew closer and closer as mother and daughter. She has always demonstrated unconditional love and treated me as her very own daughter, even though she had two beautiful daughters. Only God knew the extent of the void and pain that I carried from my mother's absence. There is a saying that goes, "There is no love like a mother's love," and my heart longed to know what that felt like. I remember a time when I was in Babies R Us shopping for a gift, and I saw a young, expecting mother with her mom shopping for her nursery. I found myself crying uncontrollably and unable to finish my transactions because it was too painful for me. I felt like I would never know or experience the joy that they shared at that moment.

I feel like when I was at my lowest point of feeling unloved and empty, God allowed Ms. Carolyn to walk into my life. She has brought so much joy, love, and affection to my life. She was there on my wedding day and for the birth of my children. Every milestone, mountain, and valley that I have had to face since God connected us, including my cancer battle, she was there. She has taught me to be an "End Time Warrior"! I will always hold this beautiful woman, Ms. Carolyn Jones Simmons, in the highest regard. I call her "mommy," and she is my love.

Message to the reader: God is always concerned about you! Know that He loves you and that He is the only one that can heal/fill your voids.

When we do the best we can, we never know what miracle is brought in our life, or in the life of another.

– Helen Keller

Celeste Terry

Celeste Terry is the Director of Grants at the United Black Fund of Greater Cleveland, Inc. She is a graduate of the Jack, Joseph, and Morton Mandel School of Applied Social Sciences (Master's Degree – Magna Cum Laude, 2003). An Adjunct Professor, and Field Instructor at the Jack, Joseph, and Morton Mandel School of Applied Sciences (MSASS), she is a recipient of the "Outstanding Field Instructor 2012" Award and was inducted into the Hall of Achievement of MSASS in 2016. Celeste was inducted into the Shaker Heights High School Alumni Association Hall of Fame, October 13, 2013. Celeste is the author of the book "Transforming Non-Profits for Relevancy in Challenging Times" (2008).

STRESS

Celeste Terry

"Come home to rest," said my mother during a phone call. I was living in New York City, downsized from my corporate job, and was temping, meaning each day brought a different work assignment – if the temp agency called. Obtaining consistent employment was tenuous. In 1988, at 28 years of age, I found a mass in my left breast around the areola. I went to a breast clinic, was examined, and told it had to come out. They suspected it was a tumor. I was sent immediately to a surgeon who tried to aspirate the mass in my breast with a needle first to see if it was a cyst.

After several attempts, the needle would not go in my skin at all – the mass was too hard. He said, "I'm admitting you to the hospital immediately for a biopsy." So, I was awake on the operating table at Beth-Israel Hospital getting biopsied. I saw the worried expressions on their faces. My surgeon came running back into the operating room, saying, "It's benign." They asked if I was alright. The tumor had started attaching itself deeper in the breast. I wanted to see it. But, they would not let me see the tumor. He told me later at my follow-up that he had a colleague at Sloan-Memorial Kettering examine the tumor to ensure it was benign. It was so kind of him to do that. I did go home to Cleveland to rest, heeding my mother's advice. There would be much more stress and anxiety as my life spiraled downward to the point where my friends were worried. After being evicted from my residence, I moved in with my dear friend John in Brooklyn, until one of my friends who had left New York City to accept a job in Miami Beach sent me a one-way plane ticket to come and stay with him to get myself together. I stayed with him for almost one year. Then when I was mentally better (still broken), I went back to John in Brooklyn for four months, then returned to Cleveland in

1992 at age 35. At age 37, there were tumors in another part of my body, my uterus, which required a hysterectomy, just the uterus. The realization that I would never have a child became clear. I wondered, "What is going on with my health? More tumors? If I don't change things, I am on my way to cancer", I thought. "I don't want a third set of tumors somewhere else." I cried in my mother's arms. She said, "If I could change this for you, I would." All this time, my mother always saved me. She always sent me money, encouraged me, and fortified me during this time when I felt like a complete failure. But I was never a failure to her. I was on my journey, and she was always there to support me – no matter what! Since I lost 80 pounds, I have been a member of a Master's Swim Group coming up on seven years. I feel good, look good, and I am happy. And one of the strongest reasons that I have been able to heal mentally, physically and accomplish so much is because I had my mother's example to watch and follow. She saved me. She bet on me - that I would make it. She placed a good bet! I survived failure. As a result of her love, she has seen me do great things. I am Ruby Lee Terry's daughter.

Turn your wounds into wisdom.
–Oprah Winfrey

Angela Triplett

Angela Marie Triplett resides in Cleveland, Ohio. She has served as the Senior Clerk for the City of Cleveland for 22 years. She is a mother of three, a grandmother of nine, and a great-grandmother of one. Angela is best described as a loving and caring person who enjoys taking care of senior citizens and dancing. She has been a member and Missionary of the New Direction Church of God in Christ for twenty-four years, where she gives leadership to the Singles Ministry and the Care Ministry. She is also one of the Founders of the Ruby Dean Huckaby Cancer Memorial Health Festival.

To contact Angela, email, ankieangelatriplett@gmail.com

HURRICANE CANCER

Angela Triplett

It was January 20, 2020, and I was excited to attend a cluster of events to honor the late Dr. Martin Luther King Jr. As my friend and I drove from event to event, our conversation was interrupted by a phone call. It was a call that I was expecting, but at the same time, not expecting because of the holiday. A nurse was on the opposite end of the line to provide me with my exam results. Life has taught me that storms come whenever they want to, whether expected or unexpected. Well, I was hit with a storm called "Hurricane Cancer."

It was a sudden and violent shaking within my mind causing a great disturbance of emotions ranging from shock, fear, and confusion as I was trying to comprehend everything being told to me. Up until that point, I had pretended to have it all together. When I hung up the phone, I looked at my friend in disbelief. She said, "What?" I replied, "I have cancer." Tears ran silently down my cheeks. She said, "Do you want to go to the church or to my war room to pray?"

I chose the war room and cried out to the Lord because I knew I needed Him. He gave me the strength to get up and drive home while I thought, "What a disaster!" I had seen this storm several times before with family and friends, so I knew the damage it could cause. After I sat in quietness, God reminded me of the conversation He had with me two weeks prior, saying I could, "Ask anything in His name and it shall be given," as well as, "You have not because you ask not." I didn't understand it at the time because the storm hadn't come yet. However, He knew what was headed my way, and I was going to need a storm shelter. I needed Him to hide me in His pavilion.

I clung to God for help and to show me what to do. I sought refuge in scripture as it pertains to healing and miracles He had performed. I then plastered the scriptures all over my house, quoting them every day so they would become ingrained in my mind and heart. I wanted to speak life into my storm, so I used the antidote God gave me. My fear turned into faith, my worry into worship, my sadness into singing, my tears into thankfulness, and my pain into praise! Would you believe the storm calmed down? I began to think clearly to schedule appointments and make wise decisions.

My surgery was on February 5, 2020. I had so much love there from family, friends, and even my Pastor and First Lady, who imparted peace while we waited. As they rolled me down the hall, I could hear the woman of God, Evangelist Janice Woods saying, "You got this." She, being a prayer warrior, called me every day to pray. She sent scriptures, motivational text messages and always had an encouraging word from the Lord. God knew I needed her. Her friendship and fellowship helped me get through Hurricane Cancer.

My recovery was awesome! I had very little pain but a whole lot of love. Every day I had visitors, beautiful flowers, baskets, and many cards that helped me prepare for the next phase: radiation. My first day of radiation was on April 2, 2020. I was afraid and emotional because I could have my two daughters with me for my other appointments, but nobody could attend this with me due to the coronavirus pandemic. I fixed myself up real pretty, repeated some affirmations, and borrowed the words of Evangelist Woods, who told me, "You got this."

Thank God for the nurses who assisted me with the 20 treatments I had to have. It wasn't always easy. Some days I would lay there and cry when that machine rolled around me, but I can hear my Grandma Jerry quoting the 23rd Psalm: "Yea, though I walk through the valley of the shadow of death, I will fear no evil, for thou art with me; thy rod and thy staff they comfort me."

On my last day of treatment, as I'm about to ring the bell, still no one was allowed to join me. I have rung the bell and began to sing, "Never Would Have Made It." As I walked out of the building, to my surprise, I heard horns blowing, bells ringing, and saw people jumping out of their cars with signs! My family and friends were there to celebrate and congratulate me for being cancer-free.

RESOURCES

American Cancer Society
www.cancer.org
(800) 227-2345

Corner Stone of Hope
(counseling services also available in other states)
5905 Brecksville Road - Independence, Ohio, 44131
(216) 524-4673

Crime Stoppers of Cuyahoga County
1215 West 3rd Street - Cleveland, Ohio 44113
crimestoppers@cuyahogacounty.us
(216) 252-7463 Tipline

Domestic Violence Center
https://dvcac.org/
24/7 Helpline (216) 391-HELP (4357)
www.hotline.org National Hotline
1-800-799-7233

Highland Springs – Substance Abuse Treatment Center
24/7 Helpline (216) 242-4505

National Center for Victims of Crime

https://victimsofcrime.org (202) 467-8700

www.OhioAttorneyGeneral.gov (877) 584-2846 (877-5VICTIM)

National Suicide Prevention

https://suicidepreventionlifeline.org/

(800) 273-7355

Postpartum Support International

www.postpartum.net

(800) 944-4773

Rape Crisis Center

24 Crisis & Support Hotline

(216) 619-6192 or

(440) 423-2020/Online Chat Available

****

For spiritual counseling reach out to spiritual leaders in your community.

WE WANT TO HEAR FROM YOU!

Higher Ground Speakers Bureau is a planning and development company built on longstanding partnerships with our clients and the community. We specialize in program development, event planning, conference management, and productions with national and international speaking opportunities.

We would be honored to hear from our readers; please write or email us and share your testimony about the encouragement that you received from this book. We hope you find transformational words in the Wounded Healer stories. If not all, we pray that at least one story will guide you to HOPE, and your healing will cause you to reach back to help someone else in need.

We welcome your prayer request! If you are currently without hope in your journey, please use our resource page to contact the organization that best fits your needs.

If you would like more information about Higher Ground or utilize any of our services, please contact us at the address below.

Higher Ground Speakers Bureau LLC
P.O. Box 603456
Cleveland, Ohio 44106
yp@higherground55.com
216-999-8573

ACKNOWLEDGMENTS

Dr. Yvonne Pointer

First, I give honor to God!

I know that there is power in words. So, with that said, I must first thank God the Father for His creation of words. The words that He loaned to us give visual effects on paper. Words can become a journey, a path for others to travel. We can read words written centuries ago in great novels such as the Bible or other books that have taken their rightful place in time and not lost the power of deliverance.

There are not enough words to adequately express my gratitude and love for the two Jacqueline's in my life, Jacqueline Williams Payne and Jacqueline Muhammad. The very sound of their names is like melodious words. They believe enough in the visionary within me to follow the vision; often blindly, I might add, but always willingly. No matter how farfetched the idea may sound initially, they are a collective force to be reckoned with and will get the job done. They are beyond friends; they are God sisters. They are Wounded Healers who continuously serve as a bridge on which I travel.

Working with Sharina George has been rewarding. She is a timely and meticulous overseer. If she says that she will do it, you can consider it done. Her company Xcellence Marketing is my go-to place when it comes to publication.

To the Twenty-Four Women who lent their words to you, the readers of Wounded Healer, in particular, my personally invited contributors; *Angela Triplett, Celeste Terry, Clarissa Foster, Dr. Jill Barry, Ilinda Reese, Jeanette Griffin, Laquania Graham, LaVerne Dawson, Linda Gamble,* and *Sharina George*. Talk about faith! Many of them had no idea what they were getting into but followed the vision, nevertheless. As a result, they crossed over into areas that were not visible from the onset.

Thank you to Shelly Shockley for her gift that opened the door for the readers in her brilliant Foreword.

To my family for tolerating my absence even when I am present, thank you!

Finally, to anyone out there who will read this book, I am grateful that you can see the vision. I pray that you will find transformational words in it and go back to lend a helping hand to those in need.

Jacqueline Payne

God organizes Divine Connections. From the beginning, God strategically connected me with people whom He has chosen for my path. He joined me to people who would add what I needed to move me further along. The favor, influence, and vision of these people flowed down to me, in turn teaching me how to return that same recipe of God's favor to others as a wounded healer.

I am grateful for my husband, Shawn Payne, who holds me up when I'm too weak to carry myself. Your words of encouragement come from God; they breathe life back into me when the transgressions of life knock me down. Thank you to my precious mother, Viola Williams, for being my first teacher. It is your faith in God's word that drew me closer to Him. My daughter Riyan - your fire, love, and grace are just an example of the spirit that flows through you; you are my most precious gift from God. Your energy keeps me alive; your smile gives me hope. To my two sons Shakir and Jeremiah, you are my extra blessing from God. Thank you for your love and support. My granddaughter, India, thank you for calling me every day to check on me during my darkest moments.

Thank you to my entire family, with whom I share my early

morning messages from God. You all were my first reach back. Thank you to my Pastors, Bishop-Elect Jamie Croone and Prophetess Tanya Croone; thank you for doing life with me.

God equips us and connects us. If your assignment requires someone else, He will ensure that the connection is made. Lord, I thank you for the favor connection to Dr. Yvonne Pointer. She is always about the Father's business. God, you made us life partners, and I cherish our sistership. To my namesake sister, Jacqueline Muhammad. I love to hear you laugh, and your soft yet courageous voice inspires me. You speak with confidence and handle God's business with grace.

"Wounded Healer" would not be possible without the brave ladies who stood with us on this journey. Thank you to all *twenty-four ladies,* each of you took a leap of faith and shared some of your most intimate secrets and your testimonies. Some of you trusted me to help you reveal the hidden words in your hearts.

A special thanks to my personally invited contributors; your testimonies will reach our readers who have wounds from life's tribulations. Because you dared to share your story, they too may have HOPE! One day they will become a Wounded Healer, just as you all are: my goddaughter *Durecia Moorer;* what an honor to witness your transformation from a young girl to a Woman of God. Your spirit is going to draw a generation of young people to God! To my Sissy *Lori Williams-Murphy,* thank you for reaching back to help young girls who were lost and insecure in the world. *Lori Middleton-Haynes,* our bond is unbreakable. Thank you for sharing the pain of losing your mother with the world at a sensitive time in your life. My dearest *Maggie Haas,* the fight in you for your son has birthed something in you that will help families across the world. *Monique Williams-Kelly,* thank you for giving back to help heal those broken little girls trapped inside every woman. To my soldier sister *Vanessa Davis*, you are a warrior for God! You can pray down fire from heaven... thank you for always answering the call. To my last wounded healer, *Minister Sheila Smith*, your love is kind and genuine, and I appreciate you trusting me with your story. I give all the honor and glory to God for each of these connections!

Jacqueline Muhammad

I thank Allah (God) for his mercy and grace for coming in the person of Master Fard Muhammad. I thank him for the Honorable Elijah Muhammad and the Honorable Minister Louis Farrakhan. It is because of these three that I have a chance to be free and to live.
A Muslim is one who submits his or her will entirely to do the will of God. Once submission is active, Allah God's will permeates through the individual. This is my life's goal.

As I live this Muslim life, God has drawn me to many people who also reflect his expressive will in their lives and their spiritual work. Two of those people are Yvonne Pointer and Jacqueline Payne. Together we have a sisterhood rooted in our love for God and humanity. We bond based on service to others. I thank God for them and our friendship.

When Jacqueline Payne sent us a text one day expressing her love for our sisterhood, Yvonne came back with an idea to allow 24 women to express to the world their love for sisterhood. And Wounded Healer was born. Putting heads together with these two dynamic ladies has been once again very refreshing.

On this journey, our first task was inviting women to participate and travel this road with us. When I came into Islam, I learned one of God's promises is to bless the Believer with friendships in all walks of life. I bear witness that God's promise is true. Yes, I have friendships in Islam, but I also have friendships in Christianity and many other faiths and walks of life. Therefore, my approach to inviting others was to share this opportunity with individuals from a range of backgrounds and circumstances. *Sister Ebony and Sister*

Sadie, you are the Sisters Allah (God) gave me through our collective MGT (Muslim Girls in Training) class. I thank him for you and our greater MGT sisterhood. *S. Cornelia,* our daughters, allowed us to find our common bond. I love you and your strength. Thank you for traveling on this journey with us. *A'bria,* I have watched you activate your love and service to girls – our future is secure with young people like you. Thank you for saying yes to participate in this project. *Charmaine & Tiffany,* we have been drawn together by a third party – I appreciate you, and I thank God for you. This journey would not have been complete without you. Thank you. *Patricia,* you share the blood running through my veins, but you also share the love of God, and that makes our bond that much deeper. Thank you for traveling with us.

For the remaining writers, thank you also for saying yes to the journey. My prayer is that every reader will be encouraged by your willingness to share your wound(s) and your victories.

To my dear mother, Jessie, for without you, there would be no me. I love you! To Sister Zandra for being my sounding board on so many topics, including this project; much love for you, my Sister.

To my wonderful, God-fearing husband, Roland Muhammad, thank you for loving me and for this love exchange we have rooted in Allah (God) that I hold so very dear. For always encouraging and supporting me and my projects. And to my children and grandchildren as well, I love you all.

Finally, we want to thank our sponsors, the St. Luke's Foundation, Third Federal Savings & Loan, Neighborhood Connections, and the City of Cleveland, who believed in the vision even before it went to print. Because of your financial support, testimonies will be captured and escorted into history for generations to read.
